# self Love
### and the
# HEALING
## of Our Animal Friends

## BETSY ADAMS

**BALBOA.**
PRESS

A DIVISION OF HAY HOUSE

Balboa Press books may be ordered through booksellers or by contacting:

Balboa Press
A Division of Hay House
1663 Liberty Drive
Bloomington, IN 47403
www.balboapress.com
1-(877) 407-4847

Because of the dynamic nature of the Internet, any web addresses or links contained in this book may have changed since publication and may no longer be valid. The views expressed in this work are solely those of the author and do not necessarily reflect the views of the publisher, and the publisher hereby disclaims any responsibility for them.

ISBN: 978-1-4525-4607-0 (sc)
ISBN: 978-1-4525-4609-4 (hc)
ISBN: 978-1-4525-4608-7 (e)

Library of Congress Control Number: 2012901203

The author of this book does not dispense medical advice or prescribe the use of any technique as a form of treatment for physical, emotional, or medical problems without the advice of a physician, either directly or indirectly. The intent of the author is only to offer information of a general nature to help you in your quest for emotional and spiritual well-being. In the event you use any of the information in this book for yourself, which is your constitutional right, the author and the publisher assume no responsibility for your actions.

Any people depicted in stock imagery provided by Thinkstock are models, and such images are being used for illustrative purposes only. Certain stock imagery © Thinkstock.

Printed in the United States of America

Balboa Press rev. date: 2/7/2012

# Acknowledgement

This work is, in the deepest sense, a Giving Back for all the Gifts I have been given by the animals, by humans, by Earth in all her Creations, Nature, and all the Beings from many Realms of Light who have helped me to Be, to Be Here, to Evolve over the years in this bodymindemotional vessel. I especially wish to acknowledge Michael Innocence for his never ending Love and Guidance on this Journey.

Dedication

This work is Dedicated with deepest Love and Gratitude to my Friend and Mentor, Michael Innocence

"It is not, really, about consensus. It <u>is</u> about honoring your Uniqueness and Lovingly Expressing this, here, now. This is true for every living being here, in This Universe and beyond. Love, self Love"

Michael Innocence to the author

# Table of Contents

# Introduction

In over 30 years of working with animals and their people one of the deepest bonds I've experienced is the depth of love and devotion of the animals for their humans, and of the humans for their animals. Whenever I have visited the animals in various settings with their human friends, or communicated with the animals and their humans, I am also struck by the deep mutual dependence of animals for humans, and humans for animals. I am using dependence in a special way here; I am meaning by it the "need for feeling loved" that is mutually present in both animals and their people. The other striking thing is the lack of self Love* that is usually present in both the animals and their people. You will notice I am using "little l" love, and "big L" Love - these are very different in their meanings and this book will explore in depth what is meant by each; and how each, love and Love, is profoundly related to the Healing of our animals friends, and of ourselves.

My life with animals and their people has been a long journey of discovering, with many thousands of teachers in the form of feathered, furry, scaley bodies as well as bodies of bare flesh. And, I have discovered that the unLoving emotions a human may have for the self has profound impact on the Health of animals. And that the animals themselves, by not Loving themselves, allow such impact. How can this be?

To explore these issues and to help answer questions relating to them, as best I am able, are the main reasons for this book, and, hopefully to help humans and animals become more Healthy, which also means to have more Love for the self.

I have always been very close to animals, since a very small child, and as an adult began working with them as an animal rescuer in the 70s. I would help the animals who were in difficult situations in the wilds, or who had critical illnesses no one else wanted to work with or considered hopeless. I took them from research labs where horrible experiments were being carried out on them, bringing them home with me from homes where they were being abused or were no longer wanted and I had been able to find a way to get them out of the situation. And more. Through it all I felt I was doing loving service to these creatures. And for sure I did not like humans very much. Ever since I was very small, about 3 years or so, I remember being able to consciously communicate with animals, in words, pictures, bodily impressions, dreams, visions, and so on. I have always just felt so close to them, and until recently, not very close to the human race. But this latter has changed. Because of the animals, and my mentor and friend Michael Innocence, as well as many humans, this latter feeling has changed a lot.

One of the main reasons for my earlier lack of feeling close to humans, even though I was living in a human vessel, was because as a small child (and all my life), I have been feeling with my body the emotions of the humans and of the animals. And while a human could be saying something with their mouth, or saying something they were thinking and believing in mentally, it could be in direct contradiction or even unrelated to what they were feeling. This conflict between the emotions and what I came to know as the ego mind never occurred in animals in all my experience with them. There can be conflicting emotions, but even these will be evident and without guilt expressed. Thus from a very young age I grew to distrust what a human was saying, what was really "meant" by them, while with an animal what they "said" to me or showed me or felt was in complete agreement with their emotional body. I felt at home and safe with animals in a way I could not do with the humans because of the human mental body (ego mind) which was not connected to the human emotional body or to the physical body energetically much of the time.

Throughout all of the rescue work one of the main feelings I had deep in my heart was judgment towards humans for all the cruelty and neglect and thoughtlessness they perpetuated on animals, on Nature. The lack of feeling in most of the humans I had come to know, for Nature and for the animals who are so deeply expressive of Nature,…. Oh, how judgmental I was! It has taken me many years to become not judgmental in this manner and to learn what it really takes to help the animals and their humans: Loving myself.

What does this mean, to Love and to Love the self? That is what this book will explore in depth, and how Loving the self leads to spontaneous Healing of the self and to those animals and humans in one's environment - if that being wants to Heal, is ready to Heal. I can say that the Healing of animals has little or nothing to do with "fixing" them, and has a tremendous amount to do with Loving them and helping them, too, to learn to Love themselves. We are all connected through our Hearts, in fact it can be said we are All One Heart when it comes to Healing. And when we Love, truly Love, we cannot judge another, or expect another to be other than they are. We learn to allow and appreciate the Uniqueness of each being here, human, animal, plant, mineral,... Hopefully this book will help in making this more clear. [1]

---

1    *Please see "But isn't Loving the self First, selfish?..." section in this book for clarifying discussion of "Love" & "love," "Feeling" & "feeling," "Healing" & "healing," and the words "uniqueness" & "Uniqueness."

# "Ask my people..." Pug & Friends!

I n my earlier visits with families and their animals I was interested in going to the home and helping the animals become healthier and happier, utilizing the various holistic techniques I had been studying along with my ability to communicate with the animals. My background in the biological sciences was also drawn on heavily, as well as my experiences in veterinarian clinics, kennels, animal sanctuaries, rescue facilities, laboratories, biological supply houses, and so on. I wanted to help the animals, and to be honest at this point in my own evolution, I had no interest at all in helping the people. This was in the mid 80s to early 90s. And at that point the people seemed to have no interest in being helped... it actually never came up until the animals brought it up!

One evening very early in my practice I was visiting a family that asked me to come over because one of the dogs was peeing all over the house, and the people were at their wits ends. They really did not want to put the dog down, the kids loved the dog, but they just did not know what to do anymore. Most of my calls at that time were related to animal behavior issues, to chronic physical conditions that were not clearing up with veterinary care, with the death and dying of the beloved family companion, or with those humans who had tried more holistic approaches in their own lives wanting to try them with their animals.

This was a family of 4 people, son and daughter, mom and dad. I remember sitting down across from them in their living room, while over in a corner a couple of cats were fighting and the dog had leg lifted and was spritzing the wall in another corner. It was very common with me on my visits that the animals "acted out" openly whatever was "up" with them; the people were usually surprised at this, but I truly just accepted that the animals were showing me how they were feeling and I was very relaxed about all of it.

As I was sitting there, there came loud and clear into my field this command, "Ask my people how they are doing!" Well, I really did not care but because it was an animal saying to do something I did it. I never questioned what an animal said or did because there was never duplicity in their expression to me energetically. And so I said, "Your kitty just asked me to ask you how you are doing?" The people all looked at me surprised, then at each other and back to me and said, "Fine!" "OK" "Cool"

The kitty said to me again, this time very loudly, "Ask them how they are Really doing!" So I did. And all of them just stared at me, then at the floor, then at each other again, and then began to tell me all about the trauma, drama, pain, hard life issues they were each having; at home, at school, with friends, and so on... All the animals at this point had stopped entirely acting out and had come to sit beside their people, on a lap, or the back of the couch, just being still and watching me.

This was astounding! And this was not by any means the last time this happened. It occurred more and more frequently, but it seems I still was not "getting the message" as it finally took one dog, Pug who was a Pug, to wake me up and clarify what my job really was with the animals at this time.

I was visiting another home, perhaps 3 months later from the previous family and maybe 12 families later. The family was seated across from me, a nice family, but again filled with the trauma and all the issues of being humans in the world and in a family. They had asked me to come and fix Pug, help him be healthier and happier, for he seemed to be depressed a lot of the time recently. They were really worried about him and I was there to do my very best to help him.

After I had gotten Pug's vet history and looked it over, and his life story as the family could remember and share, Pug came and sat down right in front of me, almost on my feet. He looked solemnly into my eyes and said, "If you won't help my people, you can't help me." This was very sincerely said with deep Truth and no getting around it! I literally cried out, loudly, "No Way!" I was really upset as I did not want to help people I wanted only to help animals! That dear Pug got up, looked at me with what at the time I thought was distain, but later realized was with great Compassion, and walked out of the room! It had happened so fast I did not have time to feel the embarrassment.

The family said, "What was That all about!?" I told them, "Pug just told me that I cannot help him if I don't help you." We all started to laugh! A lot! But then got really quiet. And then we really got down to work. At first complete consternation was the main feeling. I asked them, "Would you like my help? Do you need my help? What can I do to help?" And they all said, "Help Pug!"

And so, we were at a point in our evolution here, stuck, as we were mutually looking at Healing the animals as a separate issue from Healing the people. But Pug knew!!

I can say truthfully this was the beginning of my waking up to being human. A battle that had raged in me since childhood. I did not want to be human as I equated human with being not such nice things... however, I had to learn and accept I WAS I AM human and Pug, God Bless Him, brought this realization of my responsibility for this fact home to me. It was many years and thousands of animals and their families plus deep Spiritual work before my Heart began to Open, I began to accept myself, and I learned to Love myself and hence move into the Space of Just Being Whatever It Is I AM and Loving from This Space as best I am able. This journey is by no means "finished," for as long as there remains the feeling of being separate from the Love (ego), there is still Healing to be done.

There has not been one visit, not one phone consultation, not one lesson I have ever learned from, being with animals and their people, that has not been a profound opportunity to Open my Heart to the Love That Is, That We All Are. It has been a hard trip mainly because I was in such resistance to feeling my own pain around all that was going on in my own life and that I was projecting unconsciously onto everyone and everything in my world. I was always deeply aware of the animals' pain, but not of my own. Is this not strange? And yet, it is a pivotal energy around which growth and Healing can occur.

This pain, this pain of feeling separate from the Love We Are, is in every human, every animal, ego. It is part of the exploration here about which I will share more as this book moves on. The Earth and her Opening to the Love She Is, its impact on all living beings here; the New

Children and the New Animals arriving daily to support the Opening of the Heart... these are profound Times we are in, and the fact that we can, each of us, animal, human, all beings everywhere Choose To Be Love is the greatest of Gifts. Gratitude. God Bless Us All.

# Angel

One night in the early 90s I was visiting a family of 5 people who had 5 animals, all kitties. The family had telephoned me because of behavior issues with the kitties; fighting and again the usual spraying inside on the walls, furniture and now, the beds. By then I was doing my very best to incorporate Pug's guidance; to try and help the people as well as the animals. I was still trying to "figure out" (ego mind) how to do this... and I was discovering that in spite of myself i was enjoying more and more being with humans, with the families, sharing what was going on with them, their lives, as well as what seemed to be the "problems" with their beloved animals.

This family was having a lot of difficulty as it became clear the boy was having issues at school, being bullied, and one of the daughters was having a hard time getting her boyfriend to do the things she wanted done her way. The husband had been laid off from his work and the mother was having to start to work when before she had been a really happy stay at home mom. The youngest child just was smiley and happy and cuddled with her mom and dad.

By this time I had learned a basic element in all animal human relationships that I had experienced, i.e., that the animals mirror the emotions of the humans whether or not the humans are conscious of this or not. In fact, I came later to be able to say pretty certainly that the animals download and mirror the unconscious emotional tendencies of the humans that are making the human unhappy. In this way the human has a mirror to look into and if so desired, can become conscious of what is making them unhappy and do something about it. Choose to stay stuck in the unhappiness or become more happy. Wow! What a great deal!

In this case the mirroring of the "pissing match" between the parents as well as between the children and their own relations to parents and peers was being acted out by two of the spritzin' kitties, and actual fights were going on between two of the other kitties. And again, once we began to discuss the family issues as honestly and vulnerably as we were able, ALL acting out by the kitties ceased. All of them became calm, some going to sleep and some coming to sit on laps or along the back of chairs.

This activity pretty much speaks for itself. As I was getting ready to leave, the mother and I were standing together by the stairs that led to the upstairs rooms. Sitting very near us on the top of the post at the foot of these stairs was Angel, the pure white kitty of this family. She was just like her name, sweet, benign, peaceful, joyful, playful... all the things and emotions that were so unlike all we had been discussing earlier that evening.

The woman looked at me as said, "Betsy, how is it possible with all the negative stuff going on in our family, that we have a kitty like Angel?" I did not "know" the answer, but what was said to me loud and clear as a bell was, "You cannot have in your awareness that which you are not!" So, I passed this on from Angel to this dear lady. And we both stood there amazed, and she was really happy to be able to feel that no matter how bad things got or how bad things looked, there was angelic, deeply Loving energy in each and every one of the humans, and the animals too. Sometimes hidden, perhaps. Unconscious, perhaps. But present. For me a tremendous lesson was learned that night. And later, years and years later, as I was lying in bed one night meditating, a voice said, "The unconscious is Love hiding from ItSelf." I have come to realize that this Love is not really "hiding" but rather that we tend to be looking in another direction. (see Jung, von Franz, in Bibliography; also from Michael Innocence's papers, unpublished to date)

Angel, I came to realize later, had chosen to mirror the Love that is available to each and every living thing on this Planet and in this Universe in which we all reside for now. That she was choosing to mirror the Love That Is Prior To the sense of feeling separate (ego) from the Love We All Are; this agony and pain that lies in the core of the ego feelings about being here. We may be going through some pretty awful, dark, egoic crap, but no matter what, Love IS Here - always Present. Always. It is a matter of learning how to Feel again, to honor and acknowledge and accept how we feel egoically and Love ourselves no matter what, and the Love will burst forth Radiantly. It IS Us! It is not separate from Us. This the animals have taught me as have other humans, and especially Michael Innocence my dear mentor and friend for many years.

However, the resistance of the human to being happy, and Happy, is one of the biggest and most obvious of all the human tendencies, and I will be discussing more on this later. And I want to mention something here that is very important in the Healing process: it is not about completely "resolving" all the emotional issues of the humans and the animals in any given moment; it is about addressing them, accepting them, allowing expression of them, while feeling safe, that in every case I have experienced, calmed the mirroring activities of the animals. No self judgment, but rather learning to be in Loving Relationship to these pain filled, embarrassment filled, anger and hatred filled emotions we all have. Choosing to Love ourselves No Matter What arises from our emotional field is a most critical step in Healing.

# Prayer the Animals taught me

Early on in the relationship between myself, the animals and their people, the animals taught me a Prayer that their people can say to them, that would help the animals with regard to their own Healing; and within this Prayer was a seed of the human's Healing also. I still offer this Prayer to people and their animals. This Prayer goes like this:

"As of this moment I want you to stop downloading my stuff
i will, with the help of God, Heal myself
It is harder for me to watch (feel) you suffer
Than it is to Heal myself with the help of God"

When this Prayer is being said by you to your animal, it is important that you feel as best you are able the giving over to God of the Healing process, that you allow the Universe, Source, God, Creator... to do the Healing. It is deeply meaningful for the animal's Healing that the human "really mean it," i.e., that the human have a deep sense of commitment to what this Prayer really intends.

What has happened hundreds of times in my own and clients' experiences with this Prayer is that after the animal is asked to stop downloading the human stuff (egoic unconscious patterns, tendencies that are making us humans unhappy, all the unloving tendencies which reside within the ego/superego) there will be a 4-day hiatus (do not know why 4 days!?) where the animal really rallies, "gets better," ceases to act out or at least there is a significant behavioral change. The animal's mirroring of the human basically ceases during this time.

And then, after these 4 days what usually happens, is, I will get a call from the family that the animal has begun "getting sick again," is misbehaving again, is a bad kitty or doggy or ferret or bunny or bird or... again! And so on. What I always ask is this, generally, "How are you doing? How have you been with regard to taking Loving care of you?" And 100% of the time the answer will be something like this, "Oh! I forgot! I got sidetracked, and..." And, "Oh I've been really busy and things came up and..." and so on and so on... The "going unconscious" that is so much a part of our being.

Ultimately, as things are now on this dear Mother Earth with all the mirroring of egoic tendencies going on, the primary focus of most animal Souls is to help the human be Happy; the animals' focus is not for self Happiness, i.e., it is not geared for self Love in most cases. So, if after 4 days the humans are not Attending to "I will, with the help of God, Heal myself," the animals will revert to the old patterns of downloading in at least 85% of the cases. There are at least 15% (and growing rapidly I Feel) of the animals who are no longer downloading human egoic issues, but have turned to the Love They Are, No Matter What the human is up to. These do not include those many who are Transitioning, leaving their bodies and moving into higher realms to work in different ways. I am referring to the New Animals, who are embodied, incarnate, and here Radiating Love. Yipppeeee!

In these approximately 85% who are here working incarnate, these animals will put the human needs first, the emotional, physical, and mental needs of the human - and especially human evolution here in the ego field first. The choice to begin downloading the human issues takes precedence over the needs of the animal at every level; physical, emotional, Spiritual. Why I am not sure, except perhaps to say it is "in the Contract" between the animal Soul and the human Soul; that the animal need for self care, for self Love, are secondary to the lessons being learned by the humans with regard to these two latter.

This is pretty obvious in the case of the companion animals, it is clear that their health, their physical well being and their emotional well being are easily compromised and "given over" for human evolutionary needs - I would say in this case, the evolution is mainly Darwinian at this point, but has tremendous potential for becoming Spiritual Evolution if the animal &/or the human chooses. This choosing is based on the needs of each individual uniquely, and it is wise to not interfere, try to rush or push this evolution. When the "time is right" needs to be honored deeply. I cannot stress this enough, and have witnessed disastrous "de-evolving" consequences in people who have been pushed too hard too fast.

It is also true for the animals in general who inhabit the Earth with us humans, that human needs come first. Earth and the animals are deeply of One Heart, they reside in the One Heart with each other in a way that, because of the development of the ego mind in humans, we humans have become separated. There is on this Planet now a profound and Loving movement back to the Union in the Heart of humans and Earth, animals and Earth, through Feeling. This is a critical and wonderful transformation occurring and the integration of the human with the Heart of the One Love, of What Lives Us All, will change the human ego mind, the ego, the unconscious relationships to self, in profound ways.

There is something I want to address here, and that is the tendency of the human to feel and think they are superior to the animals. And there is a tendency in "animal people" to feel and think animals are superior to humans. Neither is in fact Truth. The human ego mind development at the expense of feeling is, in a sense, a sacrifice of the human to a kind of evolution that has brought humans to where we are today - tremendous technical and metaphysical creations and developments, but without the compassion, and yes, let's call it "humanity" that is required to have truly integrated evolution of our species. We are beings who tend to "walk around in our heads" believing our thought forms, which are generated by the ego mind and its cording into the unHealed emotions, to be who we are. It is believed by the ego mind that only by making emotions subservient to the mind will they be in our control, will we be "better people." We tend to "feel bad about" our less loving emotions and so "stuff them" down into the unconscious and sub conscious.

This activity on the part of the human ego mind is actually an avoidance of the profound depths of creation that lie within the feelings and the Love that can only be Felt when we acknowledge, allow, receive our feelings. These Loved feelings are the Healed Feelings of the unhealed emotions. This cannot be done by the mind. It can only be done through feeling and Feeling. (Please see the next section in this book)

Thus, because the animals do not have a highly developed ego mind does not mean they are "less than" humans. They are different from humans. And have a different evolution. The animals feel Earth profoundly. And as Earth, Nature, is Opening, is Healing, so too are the animals, actually more easily than the humans who are in egoic mental resistance to these changes in Feeling and feelings that the animals, Earth, Nature are experiencing. Many humans are turning to feeling and to Feeling, but the ego mind's dissolution in the Love sets up a lot of what can be called "Spiritual Healing Crises" in the humans that animals simply do not go through in the same manner; albeit deep emotional Cleansings and Surrender to What Lives Them,Love, are needed in the animals also. The animals' evolution in the feeling realms is very deep and profoundly teaching for humans if only humans would come down out of their heads and into their Hearts, into their bodies. Hearts feel in the unhealed egoic realms, Hearts Feel in the Healed Realms the Love.

So, for me, the so called dominion of humans over animals is laughable if it had not created so much suffering and unnecessary destruction and misuse of the Gifts this Earth and the animals offer. The human race is waking up to the common feelings we all have, and the wonderful teachings of the animals; more and more each day the internet is filled with stories of this bonding, photos of this bonding, this shared emotional field we humans have with our animal friends of Earth. (Please see works by Jung and von Franz also, in Bibliography)

It has taken me many years to accept, to truly realize that the animals are choosing what they have been choosing egoically, for the sake of "the Contract." I battled and battled against this fact. How hard I worked as an animal activist day and night because I felt it would "help the animals." Animal rights activists are in the millions now, and the consciousness around the rights of animals as sentient beings has blossomed and laws are changing to protect animals' Rights. More and more humans are becoming responsible for their relationship to other species on our Planet. And yet, the animals by Contract are agreeing to all the "misuse" of them - in research, in food production, in dog fights, in abusive environments all over this Earth; for medical, cosmetic, space, psychological, biomechanics... you name it, the animals are choosing to allow their bodies and their emotional fields to be invasively and traumatically utilized in order to help the human species evolve. They agree to do these things because at the Soul level they have agreed, as we also agreed, mutually, to "the Contract" which will be played out here in the ego realms (Karmic relationships). However, and this is really important to remember, "the Contract" is agreed to while in the Space of Feeling Love, of Being Love, before the Souls incarnate and come through the "ego veil" into the ego field, which is our Universe. And while in this Prior Space of Love, the animal Soul and the human Soul are singing Joyfully, "I will do Anything to Help you be Happy!" How many times I have been shown this Loving Relationship! But, once we are passing through the ego veil, we "forget" this Loving Space the Contract was Birthed WithIn. And we begin making free will choices based in feelings of being separate from this Love; i.e., we make choices based in egoic energetics. These latter choices are rooted in fear and feelings of separation from The Love We Are. And here I quote Michael Innocence: "Just because it is karma does not mean it is Spiritually appropriate." I.e., does not mean it is Loving. I will explore this more deeply in chapters to come, hopefully clarification as to what is a truly Loving Relationship to our animals friends, to each other, to Earth and all living things will develop as we go along here.

# "But isn't Loving the self First, selfish?..."

Over the years, people have said to me, "Isn't loving the self before loving others, selfish?" And exactly as I did, many years ago, they say, "With all the suffering in the world how can I be so selfish and love myself more than others?" "Isn't it more important to take care of those who are suffering, like the animals, the starving children and other humans, and Nature being slaughtered and hunted and abused and brutalized and and and..." as each of us is well aware, a very long litany of the suffering in this world.

This whole issue of "who is suffering most?" is actually not even a real issue. For we are all suffering. I remember Michael asking, "Are you, too, not suffering?" We are all feeling separate from the Love We Are. We are all yearning and seeking anyway we can to feel loved! Help! Here we are, by virtue of our egoic nature, feeling separate from the Love We Are and seeking to be loved by other egos in order to feel good about ourselves, rather than feeling good about ourselves first, and learning to Be Love and Loving First. How does one do this? How does one Love, rather than seek love in order to feel loved?

Note the capital "L" Love, and the little "l" love; they are very different energies and carry very different meanings. Little "l" love is what is called egoic love and is based on the neediness of the ego, the separate self, to get love in order to feel good about itself; another way to say it is the ego is "seeking validation of itself" from another ego, because of its inherent feelings of being unLoved. Big "L" Love is the Love of the Cosmos, the Love That IS, the Love That Is "Prior To" the ego feeling of being separate, and is everywhere, all the time, always available, always here NOW, to be Felt by each and every Heart of each and every One of Us. There is no limit to this Love, it is Infinite, and unlike egoic love, it is not "conditional," i.e., it does not change depending on circumstances such as "outcomes," "expectations," if/ then, how, when, why, who, and so on, all ways the ego, and especially the ego mind limits and conditions our experiences.

And so we can say too that there is Feeling, with a big "F" which is Feeling based in Love, in Feeling the Love Prior To ego feelings of separation; and there is feeling, with a little "f" which is egoic feeling based in feeling separate from Love, and based in neediness and the need to feel good about oneself conditionally; it is thus usually based on what someone else thinks/feels about us. To Love the self is to Love the self UN-conditionally. To love the self is to love the self conditionally, constantly second guessing one's feelings, one's motives, measuring the self against another ego and what that "perceived other" believes or feels egoically about us. These conditional feelings of love are rooted in the unhealed ego and the ego mind's judgment of the self, which is a very different thing from Feeling Love, and Being Love First, which is the true Healed State we can all Be if we would but turn to the Love That Lives Us All.

When animals work with humans, mirror humans, they are mirroring the egoic feelings that are usually unconscious and/or feelings that the human does not want to know about because these feelings make the human feel "bad" about the self. It is this avoidance of these feelings that is making the human unhappy as much as the feelings themselves; this deep resistance to feeling how we really feel. And in order to be truly Happy here in this life Now, we need to feel how we feel, allow these feelings, accept these feelings, own these feelings, and then, because Love Is everywhere All the Time Here Now, turn to this Love and bring it into the little love which is so rooted in lack of self worth and hence so needy for another to love it. And as we bring this Love in with the Breath into every cell of our body, every aspect of our being, our entire Essence - physical, emotional, mental and beyond - eventually the Love Dissolves the little love into the Love That Is, that IS All the time here anyway.

The animals mirror back to us our unhappiness as an opportunity for us to Heal. And I can say unequivocally that what happens is this: When the human chooses to Love the self First, and Lovingly take care of the self First, the animals spontaneously Heal. Immediately all mirroring of the egoically based unhappiness ceases, the animals' job of mirroring this aspect of the human ends, and the animal ceases to have all the emotional and frequently the physically based symptoms too. (In this latter case, if the body has become too weakened and wasted by the mirroring work, there may not be the energy required for total rebalancing - however the Happiness and the Joy of the Healed State will Shine through).

Another thing that I have observed happening is this, and I am seeing this more and more in these Earth Changes: the animals spontaneously Heal on their own, whether or not the humans are turning to the self Love. Many animals are coming onto the Planet now, even as the New Children are, who are done with the mirroring work of the egoic hangups of the human race. The animals are evolving with brand new frequency bands and harmonics that no longer resonate with egoic frequencies as before, although they may simply Lovingly "process" them without being impacted/impaired by these old karmic frequencies. The Contracts at the Soul levels are changing for all of us now that there is such a profound increase in the Loving frequencies pouring into Planet Earth, Her Loving Healing becoming Our Own Healing.

Another way to say this might be: The New Children and the New Animals have no interest in downloading the old egoic energies. Even though their egoic sense of separateness may not be completely dissolved in the Love They Are (it is a process), they are <u>also</u> Feeling this Love They Are, and choosing to place their Attention on this Feeling rather than tie into the egoic way of being here. I.e., the egoic way, with all the suffering and the moaning and groaning that the ego goes through because it is not getting what it "wants" what it "needs" - fulfillment by little love from another unHealed ego. These New Animals and New Children are resting in the ego sense of self that has "moved on Up" in these beings and each one is Feeling the Unique Conscousness It IS based in Love of self, of God, and Union of the once separate self with the Love It Is. Ultimately each Being will Feel complete Union with what Lives It, and when this happens is of course between the Soul and God. I Love Michael's comment in one of his papers, "One by one they will turn to the Light." Yes, turn to the Light, the Love We All Are, but have, by free will choice, "forgotten" on this journey into the ego field of separation; but will all, also Return, take the Journey Back Home.

Millions on this Planet are now doing this, animals and humans, Earth Herself, in what has come to be known these days as the Ascension process.

And another question I get a lot is this one: "Why would we even choose to do so much suffering if all this is true?" I do not really "know" the answer to this one, but I also asked this one of Michael, who said that perhaps it is just one great big experiment and exploration in what it is like to not Feel the Love one Is; what it is like to feel separate from Love. That our Souls choose to explore what it is like to feel abandoned, alone, afraid, vulnerable,... separate from the Love, separate from the self Love and the Self Love. Why would we do this? I do not know. I am pretty sure no one knows, for it may not be a "mental" thing. Feeling is based in emotions, and a lot of time emotions have no mind at all, they just "are." This is not a cop-out on my part, as I find it extremely legitimate that feelings and Feelings have great value in our lives in and of themselves, without any explanation at all.

Remember what I said back in the Introduction to this book? How my early experiences as a very tiny kid were that I came to not trust humans because what they said, what they mentally expressed often had little or nothing to do with how they were really feeling? That this made me distrust the humans? In fact, it actually terrified me, because the feelings were very very REAL to me, because I FELT them! The thoughts, the sayings, the behaviors... they were to me in those days all lies. I became wanting to only be far away from humans, and close to animals and Nature, because animals and Nature did not ever lie about how they felt.

Note that this is still all little "f" feelings. But legitimate nevertheless for a child who lived in emotions, except when she went through the fenceline that lay between where the house lay and into the Nature that was Illuminated, filled with the Light and the Love (please see my Nature section in this book). For those of us who have egoic sense of being separate from Love, ultimately, it is not possible to Feel big "F" Feelings if we do not first own, accept, feel little "f" feelings. These feelings become Feelings when we Love the self, Love our feelings unconditionally. Then there is no need to explain through the mind... we just Feel and the exploration with the mind becomes a great joy and happiness and exciting; but is not needed in the old egoic way. We are Free to explore from a very different space, the Heart Space, which has no judgment of the self. And ultimately we become very Innocent in these explorations.

Ultimately, it is our ego mind that judges. It is not the ego emotions that judge, they just are what they are, and as we all are aware we can have 5 conflicting emotions and the emotional field is fine with this; it is the ego mind that steps in and compartmentalizes, and judges the merit or demerits of given emotions. Emotions are, and as they arise they become entangled in "thought forms" that can become truly punishing to the ego, the self. To have a "self" is not a bad thing at all; to have an ego is not a bad thing. We need them in order to explore here as entities, as beings, having an experience which is unique; and so that we can discern "the other" through this apparent other's unique frequencies.

It has been my experience as I've said before that the animals do not have the ego mind so fully developed. But they do have a profound and deeply developed egoic emotional body. They too need to learn to Love the self. They too are evolving. I often ask people, do you think/feel it is Loving that the animals take on and mirror back all this suffering of the humans? How Loving is it for them to get sick with cancer, diabetes, kidney failure, become depressed, over anxious, panicky, enraged, and so on, in order to help us Heal? How would you feel and Feel if they were to "get a life of their own?!"

The animals deserve, as do we humans, to Love the self First, to take care of the self First. And then, being Love, we can All Radiate this Love to All Everywhere! Then we can all Heal, if we so choose, and the time is right. It is time to wake up, grow up, and accept we have a big ole ego, big ole superego (ego mind), and Love the self into whatever its role is in the Evolution based in Love. Time to stop shoving all those feelings down down down into the unconscious and/or projecting these feelings outward towards others, as well as inwards punishingly as we "should not have such bad emotions" we "should not be such a bad person." Time to cease expecting another ego (animal &/or human) to "save" us or "make us all better." It is time for Love, self Love. Thank You, Michael Innocence.

# It is OK to feel whatever I need to feel...

Some years ago I was in a deep emotional crisis about everything here, again. And as I have done in the past, was considering "checking out" again. I had had a very traumatic heated exchange with a friend whom I had thought really cared about me, but who had said some really harsh and not loving things to me. And, egoic as I was in that time (and still am! It's over when it's over!) I had really taken to heart all he'd said with the sharp energies that pierced my body, my heart and emotions. I was feeling a lot of pain, rejection,... the anger had not arrived for some reason as it used to do (progress!).

Well, something stepped in in that moment and said gently, "Call ___" Which I did. This man was at that time a very dear friend of mine and I trusted he could help me with this issue. When I told him what had happened, he said to me the following <u>very slowly and with deep Feeling</u>, which is to this day indelibly imprinted in my field:

"Betsy, it is OK for Betsy to feel whatever it is that Betsy needs to feel,

And it is OK for Betsy to take as long as Betsy needs, to feel how Betsy feels"*

There was such a profound relief in me when I heard and felt these sincere words from this man's Heart to my Heart. There was so much Love in these words! Up until then I had thought (ego mind) I was supposed (ego mind judgment) to feel a certain way or something was wrong with me. But NO, what my friend was saying was that it was OK for me to feel whatever I was feeling no matter what I was feeling; to allow this feeling, no matter how long it might take.

And, in those days, another condition of my ego mind was that there was always a hurry, I had to get better fast; what was wrong I was so slow about everything when it came to Spiritual stuff!? But NO, it was OK to do all this feeling in my own time, in my own unique way. Not try to be like anyone else, or live up to or down to another ego's demands on me. It was Not about consensus! And the fact that I needed "permission" to feel how I felt at that time... how deep was my sense of self suppressed and not Loved by me! I realized I need no longer seek validation of me by another when it came to my life, my feelings. What an Opening this created in my Life!

This was a huge turning point in my life and in my practices - with animals and their people and with my Spiritual practices. I had for years already been telling my clients to feel how they felt honestly and to express these feeling; and to realize as their feelings healed and were Loved, their animals would spontaneously Heal. Well, here I was getting help from a human friend on this same issue. It was not "theoretical," not "mental," but being lived in my feelings and in my body. How different this space of occupation IS! For myself and all the hundreds of animals I've had living with me over the years, I can only speculate and feel how many were really distressed, disturbed, physically and emotionally done-in, by my really deep self hatred, lack of self confidence in myself as being worthy of receiving anything that had even a hint of love (let alone Love!) in it. Oh my, what a shift was occurring when my friend said it was OK... AND for me (this is really important) I COULD FEEL HE WAS EXPRESSING HIS TRUTH, EMOTIONALLY COHERENTLY, with no separation of his mind from his body, with his mind from his emotions... It was All ONE COHERENT FIELD OF LOVING EXPRESSION! And, even more importantly for my life than even this, was I COULD FEEL in my body, my heart, my emotions AND my mind the Truth of what he shared! My whole being experienced Integration while in Relationship with another human being - mind, body, emotions All One!

This was the first time someone besides the animals, my Families of Light, and Michael Innocence, was "all together" in energetic expression of FEELING. A Human Being with Coherence! And so, I BELIEVED HIM UNCONDITIONALLY my body and my feelings accepted as Truth totally and without any question at all what he was saying to me. What a difference this Feeling of Energetic Oneness in a human being made in that moment and in all the years that have followed. The healing that occurred as to my Trusting my own body and feelings was pivotal in all aspects of Healing my Life, of learning to Feel Love as a Natural way of being here. I had "understood" this mentally, but to experience my entire mentalemotionalphysical beingness Feeling …. A profound turning point in my evolution with regard to being human myself, and my work here with people and animals and Earth and God.

How, by allowing myself to feel whatever I was feeling no matter how dark, scary, alone, hateful, angry… it did not matter what the feeling was; but by allowing myself to feel and then bringing the Love, the self Love into my being the best I could,… Oh, how my life has changed. And truly significantly and very important for me, how my animal friends have changed! It has taken time, don't get me wrong, but with this Gesture and this deep Feeling and Belief that I Want to Heal, I Want to Be Love First, whole new frequency bands of energy have permeated my body, my emotions, my mind, and I am certain of this, I can Feel this, my Soul.

It has continued to be True for me, that when I make self Loving Gestures with the Belief that they will help me Heal, I heal/Heal more deeply and my Heart keeps Opening and Opening… and I have come to realize that what is important is not the ego mind judgment around "how healed I am or not," but that I make the Gesture to Love Through All the transformative changes that occur during Healing, While Receiving Love. self Love. There is, in the Spiritual Community, the Belief that we are all Already Love, Already Healed; and this is true in the sense that on other levels, in other realms with higher frequencies, We ARE Love, no question about it. But to Be Love Here Now in this moment, and in the next moment, while embodied in a physical vessel… there is still a lot of Healing to do. The Belief that I AM Already Healed, Already Love, will eventually permeate this vessel here and in every moment. This is the New Earth calling and the Evolution that is occurring on New Earth.

My poor ego, what a beating it has taken, what a beating I have placed upon it through my ego mind and its beliefs my ego-I is never "living up to" whatever the ego mind thinks it should. What a beating I have given the world, my friends, animal and human, and plant and

23

mineral, Earth, this Universe... Well, I choose to not do this anymore, at least not consciously. The negative unconscious tendencies, as well as the helpful unconscious gifts we all have, are being more and more rapidly flushed to the surface in these times of Earth Changes, Her Receiving the ever deepening Love She Is... And we are Earth, the animals are Earth, and we are all Healing more deeply, creating a more Conscious Life here. And we can say, ultimately, Consciousness IS Love.[2]

---

2    *If you would feel helped by saying this Slowly and as best you can with deep feeling/Feeling of love/Love for yourself, replacing my name with your own, please feel free to explore.

# Nature

oday on the internet I received a remarkable photo series of Tippi, a young child raised in the wilds. Her complete union with the animals, her total lack of fear and her love of each being she was in communion with Radiated from these photos. There is absolutely no sense or feeling of separation in her from Nature, from her environment, from all the beings who are her friends. Her human parents allowed her to explore freely in Nature, trusting and open to her way of being. From elephants, to cheetahs, to huge toads, to lizards, snakes, ostrich, on and on, they are completely her True Heart Friends. I would like to be like her, I have always dreamed of being like her, and as a small child I was like her. (Please see Tippi's website, Bibliography)

When I was very small there was no sense of being separate from the Nature, from the fields, the woods, the animals that surrounded our property in the small village of Vassar, Michigan. At first too, until about the age of 3, I also felt this not being separated from my human family too. Around this age the confusion arose in me around the feelings I could feel generated by other humans, which were just like the feelings of the animals. But the human relationship to these feelings was very different than the animals' relationship to their feelings. I could feel what people were feeling but not saying, or were actually saying something contradictory to these feelings. My distrust of the humans grew.

Nothing in Nature was like this. There was just pure expression. It was all spontaneous. There was no fear in me. There was no "thinking" or "planning" or "expecting a certain outcome." Everything just WAS. And I was 100% at home with this in my body, my mind, my emotions, my Heart and my Soul. I can, as I look back, see and feel how the development of my ego mind created separation from this Union. And I can feel as I look back and observe the young girl who grew into adult hood, the battles that raged in me to return to Nature, to become One again with Her. And yet, I chose to develop my ego mind. I was in deep resistance to it, but I chose to do it. And today I accept that it was exactly what I needed to do in order to be where I am today on this dear Earth, in these amazing Opening Events that are occurring everywhere in our Universe, and beyond.

When I was about 5 or 6 I had a very large black and white cat named Snoopy, who was actually my brother's, but was "really" mine in Heart. He was my teacher and guide in those days in the wilds around our property. Every morning in the summer around 4am when the dawn was just breaking, he would come and jump on the bed I shared with my brother and sister, and would climb up my body and say to me, "Come on, let's go hunting." I would get up and in my jammies go down the steep steep stairs of our old farmhouse and out into the back yard, through the old busted wire fence and into the fields and gully with the woods. Suddenly upon going through the fence Everything Became Illuminated! The Light was so Brilliant, so Soft. And the Peace, the Quietness and the Stillness of the Breath that resides in the Heart of Nature "occurred." I was in a profoundly beautiful place, where the Light shone from within every living being, trees, birds, Snoopy, the butterflies, the grasshoppers, EveryThing Was Light within! Including my own being. For me in those days it was completely natural and I lived for these moments, the days I could be in Nature with my kittie, with All That Was all around and within me. There was, I can say truthfully absolutely no sense of separation between me, the beings, the actions,... it was truly Paradise.

The hunting that Snoopy and I would do went like this: He would say to me, "Go get me that grasshopper" and I could "see" exactly which one he wanted, so I would go get it. The grasshopper never tried to escape, but would jump onto my hand, and I would take it to Snoopy, who would open his mouth and the grasshopper would hop into Snoopy's mouth and become breakfast. There was no pain, or fight, or agony on these hunts... everything was Illuminated and Alive Always, could never "die" or "end"... but Transformation, even though I did not know the word in those days, was Everywhere All the time spontaneously and joyfully and Happily. Then Snoopy would say, "Go get me that butterfly" and I could see which one he was talking about among the many many jewell like iridescent beings that were flying about. I would go to the butterfly and put out my hand and she (or he, in this case it was a little girl butterfly) would land on the palm of my hand. I never ever closed my hand on these beings, they liked taking trips with me on my hands and my body. I would go to Snoopy, who would open his mouth, and the butterfly would very daintily walk into his mouth and he would have some more breakfast.

Then I remember one day he said, "Go get me that bird!" And the one he meant was a Happy robin way up high in the tree, and I laughed and said, "I can't get him Snoopy, he is too high up!" and Snoopy laughed with me, his deep purrrrriiieee laugh. It was only when we went back through the fence to the other side, back towards the house where the humans lived with me, that suddenly all the Light went out. I did not understand this at the time, but I was being so gently and Lovingly protected and cared for on every level. By Nature, by the animals, by my Families of Light, by God. I remember how in those days and for years after how much I loved God. How much I loved Jesus Christ. I went to church for years all by myself, and would visit every church I could to learn about the different ways God and Jesus would be in that church. When I was in Church, I would see the brilliant Incandescent white Light on the cross, never the suffering agony of a human hanging and sacrificing himself for us. I really did not believe that was what happened, although I loved reading the Bible and went to many bible classes where I memorized the Bible stories and loved winning awards... which were usually cookies or candy which I Really loved!!

Snoopy was a very large kitty and the dominant of our neighborhood. He would come home as he aged with more and more wounds, traumas to his body, his face, his jaw swollen hugely. One day he just never came back. And in the meantime many of the wild kitties around our home and from the neighbor's would come and live in our woodpile. I spent many a day playing with them, until they too "disappeared." I remember Nipper and Schnipper who were kittens I pushed back and forth in the clothespin bag as it hung from the line. But then one morning I could not find them anywhere. My parents told me they had run away, but I could feel the lying. Many kept not being there anymore, until one day I realized my parents were killing them. This created a deep rupture in my Soul's relationship to being here with beings I needed to depend on. (please see the work by Marie Louise von Franz in Bibliography)

And then one who came to mean so much to me was brought to me by my brother David, a little black kitten I named Inky. Dave brought her to me as I was sitting on the radiator in the living room in the Vassar house, crying, for that day my little calico kitten had been run over by our neighbor. He sent my friend from across the street, to tell me how sorry he was, that he had not seen Violet, had not meant to run over her. Inky became the love of my life. My link through my heart with Nature, for she was a very wild sweet kitty! In many ways she saved my life and has returned to me over and over as Jewell, always in a kitty body.

For me, when we moved from Vassar to Bay City, away from Nature, something really dark and unhappy began in me. This happened in the middle of my 10th grade in high school. We lived in a house in a row of houses far away from Nature, with no property to roam on, with a small fenced in backyard. But at least my mom and dad let me bring my little black kitty Inky, who was not allowed in the house. But of course at night she would climb up on the roof and I would open the window for her and she would creep into my bed and sleep with me and had her kittens there, and until my mother killed her was my Heart connection to Nature, the only one I had left. This all happened between 10th grade and graduation from high school. So I had had many years in Vassar, where my Heart and the wilderness could meet and merge and become One.

The reason I am writing so in detail about Nature and my relationship to it is because the animals ARE Nature. Their connection with Nature is total, and wise and a profound source of wisdom for humans to learn from, and especially to FEEL and share, if the humans can come out of the mind, that chattering ego mind, and into the body and Heart which is totally their Right and a Gift from the Cosmos to each and every one of us.

I used to wonder and beg and moan and groan big time about the fact that I was a human being in a human body, stuck stuck stuck away from Nature! But of course, this was untrue, it was just my ego's way of keeping me separate and suffering, which is its job; and in this job also providing tremendous learning and possibilities for growing, and for change. I did not HAVE to stay out of Nature. I did not HAVE to go to school and become a scientist, a biologist, and study predator/prey relationships for a PhD in Evolutionary Ecology. I did not HAVE to stop having animal friends after my family consistently killed them all or made them disappear... For some reason I chose, at the Soul level to go through this extreme separation and grief, this dark deep down and shut down way of evolving as a Soul here. Now, I am getting more and more insight into what it has been all about; but for years I was an alcoholic because I could not cope with the separation, the pain of being human when all I wanted was to merge with the feeling world, with Nature. And twice I have had the near death experiences when I wanted so bad to get out of here and go back Home; at 18 a train hit my car and at 52 I hit a tree in a black ice storm spending 3 ½ months in the hospital, with multiple surgeries and 2 ½ years on disability. In this latter I sustained a brain injury and massive trauma to my body. In both instances I was told to "Go Back, your work is not done," AND in both instances I received such loving care from humans that eventually I had to own up and admit humans were not so bad after all; a great impact on my changing attitudes towards being human myself.

It is obvious that I chose to be here in a human vessel, having human experiences. And what does it mean to be "human" anyway?! Who knows!? I sure don't. It has only been in the last 10 years or so that I became aware that I have no idea what it is to be human, not really. Or to be an animal, not really. Or to "be" in Nature, not really. I have always just been in a great big traumatic resistance to being Any thing I didn't WANT to be, or what felt like I was being forced to be, against my big fat ego will. Oh the tantrums I had as a child, as an adult,... that I had until fairly recently, when I could really begin to allow myself as best I could to own my feelings without judgment on myself. When I first began to Love myself after years and years of a blind kind of living in the unconscious and acting out without really caring who I hurt or what I did... I believe "heedless" is the correct word.

Throughout all of this the animals have been with me, have unconditionally helped me and downloaded my tendencies which were so unLoving; talking and singing and dancing and getting sick and having behavioral issues to try and Wake Me Up! Also, a lot of humans did their best to help me feel how much they loved me, the very best they could! But it was Never Enough for my ego, Never Enough… Yes, this is one of the ego's biggest mantras; no matter how much love, and Love, and Grace, and goodness and friends, and animals, and food, and shelter, and and and… nope! Never enough for me!

It has taken 14 years of what I call my Spiritual Practice and the learning to Feel the Love That Is, to Believe in and Accept That Love IS No Matter What Always available, that has broken the ego chains I allowed, I chose, to bind me. That the Love I am talking about here is Prior To everything that arises here, and any dependence I may be feeling on another egoic arising to "fix me" or to make me all better has been misplaced. Throughout all my evolution here the animals I have known and felt, have evolved, have grown, and are no longer downloading my egoic stuff at all; unless I fall into some unconscious or overwhelming trauma or grief or depression or pain where suddenly, out of nowhere there will be 7 creatures all around me, caring for me, helping me, downloading me so I can get on with my evolution (now, Darwinian and Spiritual). They all sing to me, letting me know All is OK! You Can DO this! Give it Up and Hang In There… But most important, over and over, singing TURN TO THE LOVE YOU ARE TURN TO THE LOVE YOU ARE And now I, too, sing this to myself naturally. Oh! How the Mirrors are Changing on this BeLoved New Earth!

These days, and for the past 27 years I have lived on a parcel of wilderness with a mile long drive off a dirt road. I maybe brush hog the field once a year if I feel like it. The woods surround this property, the entire place here filled with Light. The animals visit constantly, fearless, all kinds, all times of day or night, openly here in broad daylight, the coyote, the deer, the skunks, the cooners, the possums, vultures, all kinds of birds and critters visit or maybe stay awhile, move on to whatever it is their Life here to move on to… I am holding onto nothing anymore. It just IS, and I am in It, in Nature imbued with the Love, from which ultimately All Arises, from which Nature Herself, Earth Arises. The Gratitude. This is the major feeling I have, even for my dear ego whom I Love profoundly. Gratitude. For my Life, for my Breath, for the Cosmos and the Love It Is, and that I am a Unique Arising of. Nature holds the Love of the Cosmos in a profoundly Loving manner, holds Us, all creatures forever, for we Are Nature, Healing. How could it be otherwise? I Love You.

# Evolution

We could say there are, essentially, two kinds of evolution going on simultaneously, Darwinian and Spiritual. There are significant differences between these two types of evolution and their impact on animals, humans, Earth and this Universe we all reside within.

Darwinian evolution is based on demonstrated factors that impact population numbers: limited resources and the necessary genetic production of bloodline offspring in competition for these limited resources. It is easy to feel how Darwinian evolution is egoically based, for the ego is replete with the feelings of "never enough" and issues around survival, reproduction, and the need to control outcome relative to these survival issues. Darwinian evolution is focused on the body and its physical, emotional and mental constituents as being the identity of the being. There is, in essence, nothing beyond this struggle for survival of the bloodline through the wonders of genetic mechanisms that may or may not have value in terms of survival for a given species. The importance of the individual, per se, is negligible except for that individual's contribution to the gene pool and offspring survival. (please see Brune in Bibliography)

Spiritual evolution is based on the belief that there is more to life than just this limited vantage point of survival and competition for limited resources. There is an assumption in Spiritual evolution that there are unlimited resources, infinite abundance, endless supply of all that is supportive of life everywhere without the need for competition. That this does not seem, from the egoic viewpoint, to exist in the "here and now" has led to various afterlife scenarios in which the above is true. Many would say that we are actually "Remembering" our previous, Prior State, existences. There is also in Spiritual evolution an identification with "Something" that lies beyond the individual who is so limited in the Darwinian definition, from which Everything Arises, is Created.

We could say that Spiritual evolution looks upon Darwinian evolution as the consequence of the ego-I's essential sense of feeling alone within itself; as being a separate identity, separate from every other ego-I here in this realm. So, carrying this further we can say there is an encompassing of Darwinian evolution within Spiritual evolution, where the former is viewed as the evolving of species who feel "cut off" from the Infinite Abundance, Loving Support that is actually available to all, all the time. Because of the ego-I's sense of being all alone within its own body, mind, emotions, there develops the seeking on the part of the ego-I to not feel so alone; this vulnerability on the part of the ego-I is at the crux of Darwinian and ultimately of Spiritual evolution. For, within this vulnerability, in which free will also resides, the ego-I gets to choose whether to explore here on Earth from a sense of feeling cut off, and hence fear based exploration; or to choose to explore by Feeling beyond this limited fear filled experience, to the Love from which it is Birthed and to which it ultimately Returns.

So, vulnerability and being vulnerable and expressing vulnerably... what does that feel like when we remember our lives, or observe and feel how people and animals treat each other here in this "ego field"... in this place we all share, that has evolved based on feeling separate from the Love We Are? In this place where the brutality to the bodymindemotions is a way of life? How would it feel to be vulnerable when you are a human child being abused, or a steer going to slaughter, or a kitten being stomped on, or a young man or woman going to war, or being CEO of a large corporation managing other people's wealth, or being dropped on the ground by your father, your mother,... On and on and on, the lack of feeling safe enough to be vulnerable, to express vulnerably, is deeply embedded within the ego; for two major reasons. One, the initial coming through the "ego veil" from the Prior State of Feeling Love into manifestation while incarnated in a physical vessel, with its resulting shock and trauma and fear at this "separative" process (which happens over and over until the Soul's evolution in the ego field is "done"). Two, as a consequence of lifetimes lived in this "contracted" fear filled space (the ego in the ego field) and those free will choices made while believing this state to be true. All of this latter is accumulative, and creates karma; and as we are all aware, karma holds within its meaning, having to come back and balance, rectify, what has been created by the Soul, its vessels, in the ego field. All of this is founded in free will, but the forgetting that occurs when the being moves through the "ego veil" is built into the Soul's agreement to be here, in this place so "cut off" from what we Really Are: Love.

And yet, I remember the story by Krishnamurti, an Enlightend Being who lived in the late 19th to the mid 20th centuries. He was seated in Meditation with his followers, and he said, "For years now you have followed me, listened to me, been with me. And yet none of you has changed." (my interpretation of this is, that none had become EnLightened, Feeling Beyond the separative feelings of egoic identification). The other story about Krishnamurti affected me profoundly when I read it in the 80s, where as a young boy he was sent to school with his brother in India, and day after day after day he was beaten by the teacher. He would stand and the tears would be streaming down his face, and then he would walk home with his brother, only to have this process repeated for YEARS! His father kept sending him back to this brutalizing teacher. Krishnamurti's response when asked about this was, "You see, it did not change me." You see, he was Love, he Felt Love Beyond the physical and emotional abuse perpetrated on him by this other human form. He did not identify with his body, his emotions, his mind. He Felt Beyond them to What Really Lived Him. Love. He never, ever stopped Loving. Michael Innocence is like this, Just Loves, no matter what pain he is in, no matter what atrocities are in his Awareness, or are happening around him, or he is processing. He Feels Beyond to the Love He Is, in every moment, Surrendering to This, The Love That Lives Him. He is not changed by what arises here in this Universe, this ego field.

Another amazing thing about our evolution here is that we come into this ego field completely physically vulnerable and dependent on other beings in all ways. The infant as an opportunity for the human and the animal to be in that vulnerable space with another, with a being who can be of no harm physically, mentally, or emotionally... how does this feel? And how does this Feel? To relax, to be still, to calm down, to lie down in a safe space, to become completely Trusting that you will be Lovingly cared for and protected no matter where you are, who you are with... these are truly core Feelings that come to all when we turn to the Love We Are. All Is Provided For on every level. These feelings we have as ego for the dependent infant, are a profound opportunity to connect to Feeling the Love That Is Prior to the ego. And these Feelings are always available whether with a kitten, a puppy, an infant, a flower, a stone, a gem, another adult human, ... no matter what or who is arising here, we can Feel Beyond to the Love that IS, for There Is Only Love, ultimately.

For my own self and all the trauma my self has created here based on the fear of potential harm, loss of my "integrity," real or imagined damages to my wholeness as a unit in this ego field... When I feel the coming into this ego realm of the infant animal or human or plant; that this being has chosen to trust, to place its body, it opening being, into the care of another egoic being... herein lies for me one basic Gesture of Trusting that can carry me deeper and deeper into full Surrender of my body, my mind, my emotions to the Love That Lives Us All.

And in those moments when I am happily exploring what makes me happy, and relaxed, and just being here; when I am serving or exploring the wonders that arise in this realm endlessly... in these moments, too, if I but Remember the Feeling of Being Loved, if I can turn to these Feelings of Love that are also Me, MySelf,... Slowly but surely, and gently and Lovingly, there is an Opening Opening of my Heart, my body my mind my emotions that spontaneously occurs. I need do nothing but rest in this Space of Receiving the Love I Am, and in this Receiving I am also Giving : to myself, and to every being I come into contact with. I am in resonance with What Lives All and hence is available to All.

Thus, even though we are born into the Darwinian creation we have all made here with our free will choices based on fear and separation and seeking, we can ALSO in each moment be Feeling Beyond this, to the Love We Are. Darwinian evolution is a magnificent awesome creation and the creatures that have evolved here over the millennia are astounding. We are among these creations, and I believe we have incarnated here over and over during these creations. I also believe that we are Souls who are choosing to explore Darwinianly. I believe that karma is essentially the consequences of exploring based on free will choice a Darwinian way of evolution; in lives based on the belief we are limited, alone, and must compete for limited resources. We choose to explore here; and we can at any time incorporate into this exploration The Feeling Beyond this Darwinian experiment.

It is not hard to feel how different the impact on an animal, on a human, on a plant, on Earth and other beings within our Galaxy and within our Universe would be, depending on the belief grounded in egoic separation &/or Spiritual Oneness. The necessity to Feel Beyond the egoic arisings in this ego field to that State Prior To ego, is required for true Spiritual evolution to occur. And the changes that occur within the beings who Attend to, and Receive, this Love are profound, and impact Darwinian evolutionary states at all levels of existence here. This is, for me, one of the most important reasons for turning to the Love We All Are. The ego by its very nature, cannot Heal itself. It can by its nature and evolutionary development gather insights into its mechanisms, tendencies, patterns; this is what psychological and psychoanalytical studies and support are about. But these latter cannot Heal the egoic patterns, for the egoic patterns are rooted in the feeling of being separate from What Lives It. The ego, by its functional definition has a dedicated mission to "being separate," to feeling separate, to supporting evolution of a species and individuals within its limited viewpoint. The ego and its ego mind cannot afford to Feel infinite abundance, unlimited resources, Oneness, the Prior State Love, for then (it believes) it will "end." The mind and its self-generated "beliefs" are another issue all together, and have essentially nothing to do with Love. The mind is rooted in the "need to know" and thus Metaphysics is rooted too in this need to know, to explain, to explore... Metaphysics is not rooted in Love, in Feeling. I enjoy immensely exploring Metaphysics and the mind oriented and created Wonders... but I believe the Void is the ultimate domain of the Mind, and of Metaphysics. The Void does not Feel, but holds Potential, and can ultimately when Infused with Love, Open as the Heart Opens to the Infinite Expressions and Creations of Source. Metaphysics and explorations rooted in mind (and Mind) is for me an amazingly fascinating Realm; but Love FEELS, Love is FEELING and it is interesting to "conjecture" (mind) what the True Relationship between the Void and Love Really IS!

Now, to return, the ego, because of its identiy with the bodymindemotions, believes it will "die" when its vessel dies. This ego-I identity with the vessel is crucial for Darwinian evolution to occur; that through acquiring maximum resources and producing through bloodline offspring is the ego's primary and for all practical purposes, only way to "immortality." What is wonderful in our journeys here creating Darwinian evolution is that immortality may be seen as occurring in other manners… beings such as Brahms, Shakespeare, Einstein, Freud, Darwin, and many many other beings have gained immortality through their creations that are available beyond the biological reproductive unit at the core of Darwinian evolution.

And then there is Hubble! How this creation has brought us all together, the Universe at our doorstep! I remember the frisson of joy I got when at the end of one of the programs as part of the Universe series, the moderator said, "We love our Universe." He said this with great tenderness and awe and truly Love. How the physicists and astrophysicists who are involved in this work of discovering the Universe at so many levels are animated, jumping up and down, excited, feelingly relating how they feel about this amazing and beautiful and unexplainable Universe we live in! There is so much feeling in them! And when I Feel and feel these beings it is the dissolving of the egoic love in the Love, the egoic mind in the Love…. these beings, even though they are expressing mathematical theorems and describing "how" things work in the Universe, I do not get the Feeling they feel separate in these moments of great joy and sharing with us all the love they have for the Universe. The Love they are becoming and Radiating as the Universe ItSelf.

Spiritual evolution at its Heart, does not Feel, or Believe, anything is separate from anything else; that separation is, in fact an illusion, a delusion, of living within the egoic mechanisms here. The fact that I am sitting here, now, writing all this down has a strong possibility of separation in it. But what is my Relationship to the words that are coming forth? As I feel, and Feel this, I can say it is both; my ego mind is working away making sure it is all coming out right on the page but there is a deeper relaxed Surrendered Relationship to it all, to the process of creating this being, this book.

One of the things that Michael Innocence has said that profoundly affects me is that (and I am paraphrasing a bit here) people have misconceptions about what the ego is. He says that the ego might be considered as simply the body mind which will never disappear as long as we are alive. The problem, he says, is with what Michael calls "the contractive ego," which is the tendency of the body mind to withdraw from the field of relationship, from the Universe.

This problem, the contractive ego, or the tendency of the body mind to withdraw from the field of relations and the Universe; what creates such contraction? I am going to venture to say here, and I could be wrong, that we contract as consequence of the initial impact of coming through the ego veil and in conjunction with exploring here in this dense ego field while feeling separate from What Loves Us All, feeling unLoved, and vulnerable and unsafe while identifying with the bodymindemotions. The feeling here in our world that there is the need to compete for resources, compete for mates, compete in the Darwinian sense, which would result in contraction of the vulnerable self away from relationship with others here - going so far as to destroy, damage, kill the "perceived competitive other." And if we believe that what is here is all there is, and what is here depends on our competitive skills and developments, we are each creating a contracted ego-I away from each other and What Lives It. One of the major consequences of this energetic contraction is the need for power over another in order to feel safe, the need to control outcome, to be in charge, in an attempt to assuage the fear of another's taking over the vulnerable ego-I.

This vulnerable ego-I, when it feels incapable of competing or of "living up to" some other ego's expectations, demands, cohersion, can actually turn on the self in extreme self damaging manners; emotional suicide, as well as actual physical suicide, being the most extreme cases. (please see Bergler, Bruner, Weininger, Jung, von Franz in Bibliography)

This is a sad scenario, but one most of us here feel to be the "way of life" here. We will know and Feel we are Divine when we transcend this whole theatre of fear- based, unLoving, self-motivated desire for "egoic satisfaction" within and without. Each of us is a unique arising, there is no other being exactly like us in any of the Universes. With Loving Care each can become a truly Unique and Healed Arising in alignment with what Lives It. It is not at all about consensus, but about learning to honor each being's unique (and ultimately Unique) offerings, and this applies deeply to honoring first one's own uniqueness which with Loving tending can become one's Uniqueness here.

# That Famous Triad

That famous triad, "victim, perpetrator, rescuer" is energetically at the heart of our egoic relationship to each other as humans, as humans in relationship to our animal friends, and in our perception of animals to animals. The need for the ego, as early as 3 months of age, to feel good about itself is so indelibly imprinted that it will do many self damaging things to itself in order to have the approval of another (ego), &/or will do many self damaging things to itself in order to continue to suffer, to have that psychic masochistic pleasuring that resides deep within its core mechanisms. (See Edmund Bergler's publications, bibliography)

I want to reiterate here that it is my own belief that we are not our egos, we are in fact something "other" that we have forgotten about by agreement, by "Contract" and that coming here to Earth is a profound exploration and opportunity to learn when "cut off" from the Truth, i.e., that We Are the Love Prior to ego, Prior to this ego field we reside in, this ego Universe we are co-creating all the time. We are not powerless, we have free will, we are not victims, we are not without many means to help ourselves Be and Be Here Happily; not replaying the old "victim, perpetrator, rescuer" dramas that are manifested through karma.

It ultimately takes Wanting to Wake Up, Wanting to become Conscious, Wanting to be Free of the ego with its built in feeling of being separate from What Lives It. The Returning Home we are all hearing about so much now, and many are sharing in - the Ascension process, which is basically Waking Up to the Love We Are while being fully embodied in our physical vessel; not leaving the body in order to Feel this Love. We are choosing to bring Love, and hence Healing, into this Sacred Vessel we inhabit, and clarifying through Feeling Love, the self Love, and dissolving the ego in this Love We Already Are, Prior to being "shut down," stuck, victimized, damaged... you name it, ...that the exploration here in ego separation has created and perpetuated with our agreement for millennia.

This Waking Up includes Waking Up to our relationships to animals and humans, to our relationship to the Earth, the Universe and the many inhabitants within and beyond our Universe. The writings by Edmund Bergler, especially his Introduction to the work, "Principles of Self Damage" as well as the whole of his book, "Curable and Incurable Neurotics" are to me, must reads for insight into the depth the hold the negative unconscious ego and super ego mechanisms have on us all, and hence on our animals. No, the animals are not Free from ego, not at all, unless they are Choosing as Souls to come into the ego field as Free (some of the New Animals). The trillions of animals here, now, in service to the humans and to Planet Earth are in egoic bondage by choice, just as we are. They too are tied into the famous triad, have Chosen as we have, to be tied into being victims, perpetrators and rescuers. It is what the animals on the Soul levels are choosing to do as long as the humans and Nature and Planet Earth (Who Is Us) choose to live in this triad of unLoving energies.

I want to say here that I believe none of this is about "being guilty," about taking a guilt trip around all that is happening here; guilt is part of the unHealed egoic structures tied into the unresolved issues of the infantile ego. Guilt has no part in Love, in Loving; and hence there are no feelings of guilt when we are Healed. But the ego, with its judge the super ego (ego mind) really "gets off on" the suffering that resides in feeling guilt. It is a huge part of our evolution here as humans... the vast majority of religious doctrine relies heavily on guilt and something called "original sin" which keep the humans unhappy and in the hamster wheel of ego/super ego creation of the triad. I am not saying this doctrine has been created with Consciousness; and in fact would say most of it arises from unconscious beliefs residing in the infantile ego/super ego structures rooted in fear and based on the sense of being separate from Love.

Animals will mirror ANYTHING that is emotionally making us unhappy. This is a fact. I personally have observed and worked with this thousands of times now. It is a job the animals have chosen to do, before incarnation, while Feeling the Love They Are. And with them, it is an exploration we have chosen to do, before incarnation while Feeling the Love We Are. A Mutual Contract of "I will do Any Thing to help you Feel Happy!" is the mantra Happily shared with Hearts Wide Open in the Space of Feeling Love, Being Love... Before the stepping down energies of the manifestation chambers, down down into this extremely dense ego field where I am writing this to you now. This really dense place where we all feel cut off from What We Really Are.

No one here is in fact a victim. We have got to just get used to this fact, and Love ourselves through it. Not even the animals are victims, although the ego really loves to get wound up in this one! My ego sure did, for most of my life and I still fall into that egoic entanglement which is part of our exploration and learning what consequences of making unconscious choices are. Learning to make more conscious choices as we move back up, up, up the frequency bands and fields that permeate this ego field, moving more profoundly into Home, Love, self Love.

While in the ego-I with its infantile emotions, we are constantly creating victims so we can be rescuers and thus feel better about ourselves egoically (we are, in fact the "victim" we create "out there," projecting onto the world and into our relationships our own feelings of powerlessness that lies deep in our self). We are constantly creating and being perpetrators so we can feel bad about ourselves and fall into that deep dark psychic masochism at the core of our self, &/or again projecting onto the world unconsciously many of the unHealed self-damaging emotions we feel about our self – blaming others for what we cannot face in our self, do not want to know about our self. And then we all want to be the rescuer, yes? The one who comes along and saves the victim from the perpetrator(s); again the internal battle within our self being projected outward unconsciously.

The lack of Feeling Love, or even of feeling love, for the self, for the ego and its ego mind is what keeps this internal, projected, triad alive within and "out there" in the "perceived world that lies outside the ego-I".... And in this hall of resonating mirrors, each of us merge with, and shares harmonically resonating frequencies that keep it all alive - "out there" while at the same time simultaneously resonating "inside." We are profoundly creative beings! Would that we were Creating bridges and means of Feeling Love for our self, self Love for our self, rather than continuing this self and "perceived other" damaging ego dance.

For me, the hardest is the whole predator prey drama* of this ego field. I bring it up because of how deeply it has impacted my life here on every level of being; and my life on many other levels of being. I went to school for a PhD in Evolutionary Ecology and studied predator prey relationships for this degree. I did not finish the degree, but spent almost 5 years studying this area as I was obsessed by what I felt in my body as the brutality, pain, agony, of the prey while at the same time could feel the ecstasy, excitement, thrill, conquering energies of the predator. I was unable to egoically "disengage" myself at all from this drama that was playing out in every aspect of my life : in Nature, in my relationships with humans and animals, in relationships between my animals and other animals, in the world between other humans, other humans with animals, humans with Nature... there was no quarter in time/space of my existence where predator prey relationships did not crop up, appear, manifest. This had been going on since I was a very tiny kid! (please see Nature section of this book)

From my vantage point now, when certain energies permeate existence in such a manner, this is a big karmic issue; a big "Lesson," a big exploration, that I had come to this Earth and this ego field to partake in. That I chose to partake of this I have no doubt. And the fact that the first memories I have of Nature, of being in and with Nature, was in the fields and woods with my kitty Snoopy who early in the mornings would come and get me, saying "Let's go hunting." In the Nature section of this book I wrote in detail on this continuing experience throughout my childhood. The Light, the Love that permeated these "hunting expeditions" was nothing like what I feel when the Light, the Love is not present. It is this "conflict" between FEELING the LOVE of the predator prey for each other in these Light and Love filled experiences, as compared to when the "Light goes out" or is no longer present that permeates the egoic experiences. This egoic "conflict" has never yet been fully resolved in my existence here. I tend to be either in the Light/ Love OR in the egoic relationship to predator prey. However, I have also been in profound UNION WITH the LOVE permeating predator prey relationship during which I can also Feel my ego, my separate self, which at these times has no impact or power. The ego and its unLoving relationship is just present, I observe it, I Feel and feel it, but it has no power to disrupt the Meditative Space of UNION. I can Feel in the

Meditation the Healed predator prey, I can Feel the Love of predator for prey and prey for predator; they are ONE. I can FEEL this in my body, my Heart, my emotions… there is no separation, no agony, no "death," no ending for either. There is just Transformation.

But when I am focusing more from my egoic energies, and I am still in these energies here on Earth in this Universe, I feel the separation, the agony, the death, the dying, the battle to <u>not end existence of this separate "unit," the self</u>. I can feel the body as it battles against its ending, as the consciousness And the unconsciousness of the prey battles against this ending of the Union of Soul with Sacred Vessel. I can feel in my body the ecstasy of the predator in its "killing" of this other being; is it partaking in an ecstasy of Release also? For always there is the Surrender of the prey to What Lives It, even though the ego of the prey battles for its existence separate from What Lives It - this separate self, that must at any cost remain separate, for that is its job. Predator prey for me is the most difficult for me to "hold" …

Yes, that's it! To Hold Stably the Feeling of UNION. I have been able to be in Meditation with the animals during predator prey activities, which is definitely another book; but to remain IN this Loving Relationship, to HOLD IT, BE IN IT Constantly, Forever, I just have not been able to do this yet. I keep "falling back" into the egoic separative state … into the battle against surrender of my separate self to What Lives It… which of course, results in the famous triad energies of "victim, perpetrator, rescuer." One day, One day God Willing…

Thus, for me at least, perhaps the Lesson is to Hold the Love, the Feeling of Union With the Beloved no matter what is arising, no matter how traumatic to the egoic sense of self the event is producing within my ego. And since I am a very emotional person, and my ego sense of self is very present emotionally; and since I really feel my body and impressions within my body of ongoing emotional energies, my relationship to trauma here and Being Meditated Lovingly through the traumatic event has been really difficult. It is a whole body, a whole emotional field issue for me; not mental. I cannot leave the body and go mental anymore. I cannot detach from the emotional field in my Being Meditated by God, by the Beloved. So while I am Being Meditated I am <u>also</u> feeling whole boldily, emotionally, all that the ego is going through during predator prey activities (as well as all the multitudinous traumatic events which occur here in this realm). There has developed, for now, this "dual state" in which I feel everything going on in my body, my emotions along with a "disengagement" from these that is Created Spontaneously by the Love permeating my vessel.

As a child I did not avoid any of it. My emotional field was wide open to the Light, to God, to the Meditation, bingo! There was no having to "focus on" or "Attend to" the Meditation; It Just Was … and then as I grew older, and especially as my (remember this was my Soul's choice) animal friends were killed and kept disappearing, the Light went out more and more and I began to feel less and less, and to Feel less and less. It was just too much pain for me to bear. Being moved away from Nature and the killing of my kitty Inky by my mother was the last straw until much later in my life when I met Michael Innocence. I was deeply in the dark places of egoic separation and hate for the humans (myself), along with deep into being the "rescuer" of animals from the hated humans when I met Michael. In fact the first time I met Michael Innocence was in the dream time in 1985, when my doggie Lady was dying.

At this time I had around 50 kitties, 5 doggies and several wildlife living with me. In the biggest room at the back of the house I had set up the "critical care" room for animals who were wounded, critically ill, dying. I slept on a mattress on the floor in this room. And as I lay beside Lady, she and I rested by the doorwall windows that looked out towards the big red barn and the woods to the North and East. It was November, and very cold. It was snowing. I had brought Lady in from the barn; the other doggies were safe and snug in their deep straw beds in a cozy space, and could romp and play in a very large space. I had been at work on the afternoon shift at the hospital's automated chemistry labs and was exhausted. In those days I slept very little as I pretty much worked 24/7 making money to help animals, and then worked with my own animals, plus did rescue, and animal activist work.

Lady, a lab shepherd mix, was a rescue I had gotten from the middle of express way median at Telegraph and I94 near Detroit with Red, her companion, an old Springer Spaniel. She was a puppy and Red had picked her up somewhere. They were roaming the freeways, and Red never did get over his roaming ways! Now, some 7 or so years later, Lady was dying and was whining and whining to be with her buddies out in the barn. I was really tired and cranky and said, "Lady will you shut up!" and "bink!" something tapped me on the head just above my forehead. I "passed out" and could feel and see myself leaving my body, as was Lady, both rising out of our bodies through the tops of our heads, out through the doorwall windows, and into the most Beautiful Colors I had ever seen since childhood! Brilliant soft Glowing Reds Blues Yellows Greens Crystalline Flowers and Trees Butterflies Dragonflies Vibrant Vibrant and Lady and I were running to the Barn, filled with Joy!! Laughing and then, Lady raced into the Barn to be with her pals!! And there in the doorway to the Barn was this Beautiful Being, Radiating Love I had never Felt in my existence here. He was dressed in an irridescent indigo blue tight body suit... like a space suit! Even in this Vision Dream I was amazed! I blurted out, "Who are You!!?" and He said, "Betsy, I am Michael, and I am here to tell you that You and Your Animals will always be taken care of." There was such Love radiating from Him! I thought he must be Arch Angel Michael. I went into the Barn with Michael, and as we stood together all the doggies were playing and just being Happy! Lady was completely healthy! All Felt completely Natural. I had nothing but awe for this Being, Whatever He was. I felt no fear at all with him, just this "recognition" of Love Beaming at me! Michael took my left hand and we began to walk out of the Barn, and I said, "Michael, I'm afraid of Sex." And Michael said, "I Am your Angel." And I said, "What did you say?!" And in this dream we turned to each other, and he took my other hand in His and gazing with the most profound Love I had ever Felt in my life here, He said, "You Are My Angel." And bink!, that tap again... I woke up! And Lady woke up! There she was, lying beside me just like before we met Michael. Only now she was smiling and her tail thumped and thumped the floor! And I said to lady, "It is OK for you to go Lady, You will be taken care of." And I fell into a very deep sleep. When I awoke, Lady had died. Michael had come for her and had so Lovingly taken her Home! I did not stop weeping for a long time.

This meeting with Michael in the dreamtime, this Loving Being occurred in 1985. I met Michael Innocence in person on Earth in 2000. 15years after my dream of Him. He has never ever been anything but Loving to me, no matter how screwed up I was, have been. I want to be like Michael Innocence. And no matter what, in all the years since, I HAVE been taken care of, and all my animals HAVE been taken care of. Lovingly.

When I said to Michael, "Michael, I am afraid of Sex." You will notice that there is a capital "S," this is the way it was in the dream. Divine Sexual Union. Union with the Beloved. i.e., the dissolution of the ego in the Love that Ultimately Lives it. The little "s" sex that we all really want to experience here in the ego field, while feeling separate from What Lives Us... the orgasm is known as "the little death." I am not sure of this, but I believe that it is during the union of two loving egos in sex (orgasm) that the most profound possibility of Feeling the Beloved occurs. Because of the trust and vulnerability that occurs in the loving embrace, one is able to surrender to the feeling, which because of its intensity and the depth of surrender of one loving ego to another, can become Feeling; a shared Feeling of the Beloved, although temporarily. One of the sayings by Spiritual Teachers is that when they are Being Meditated by God, the Beloved, it is like having a constant orgasm. Sexual Union with the Divine, how deeply this calls to us no matter what stage of evolution we are in. I am sure it is "programmed" into the ego self so it will remember Home in a most astonishingly beautiful way!

This profound Vision Dream with Michael was far more Real to me than my daily life; and over the years I have had many of these Vision Dreams with Michael in which he helps me to have insight into my ego patterns, and helping me with becoming Free from the ego and its way of life here. One thing that has been a deep goad for me is that whenever I am feeling happier, even if it is egoically happier, my animals always display more health and happiness.

To do this Spiritual Evolution strictly for me, for myself, has been impossible for me. And here I need to confess what is probably my major most self-damaging unconscious egoic tendency: to overserve at my own expense. Always, if I am not in service in some way, I do not "feel good" about myself; and so, as unLoving and un-nurturing as this behavior has been, even during Spiritual Waking Up, it has had dire consequences.

It took being told by doctors a couple years ago when I was dying with congestive heart, that if I did not stop everything I was doing and take care of myself 100%, I would not be here, I would die. Well, I did not want to leave the body, and so have been doing my very best to learn to Love myself no matter what else is going on in my life. It has become my biggest desire to Be Love First and to emanate This Love, to Radiate It in every moment. And then the animals, and the humans, and Earth, and all that lives everywhere need no longer be in resonance with my unhealed egoic mechanisms, but with a Healed Being. The fact that my animals have done nothing but get healthier and happier the more deeply I Feel Love and Am expressing Love, has become a tremendous help (goad) to my own Opening to God.

And, as I am more and more Lovingly taking care of my self, I find I do not have humans coming towards me now who are so life negative and dependent and living so deeply in the Famous Triad. The people I am meeting and sharing with, and this includes clients, their animals as well as generally, are really interested in dumping the old ways of being here, ye ole: victim, rescuer, perpetrator. I am Feeling more and more I just need to stay in this Surrendered, Receiving Love and Giving Love Space and All will Heal. I don't need to "do" anything, fix anything. Everything here has built into it the ability to self Heal if we but turn to the Love We Are. I have decided that I do not want, under any circumstances, the animals downloading my egoic stuff; I will Heal myself with the Help of God, the Beloved. I do not want my animal friends holding onto the old Triad, but to release it Lovingly. Ultimately, God IS, Love IS. It is just that I need to keep aligning with This. So I do. [3]

---

3    *Along with this I wish to include the utilization of animals in research, of humans in research, for the sake of the ego mind and its need to control by gathering information at the expense of honoring the feelings, the emotional and physical integrity and the uniqueness of each being here on this Planet, in this Universe. I have since the 60s been involved in this arena of our egoic lives here and am doing my very best to bring Love into every aspect of it. Two books, "The Sacred Body Factories" and "Letters To The Animals" deal extensively with issues of creation, transformation, utilization, and etc. of the Sacred Vessels all beings inhabit. Both books will be published soon.

# MoonBoy & Tramp Part 1

**M**oonBoy and Tramp became connected through a miraculous kind of experience in my life that I would like to share with you. It is the sort of occurrence that keeps coming into my life more and more and for me enhances my already deep belief that what the Universe has in store for me I need to Surrender to, not battle or resist. All is as it Needs to Be. Now.

Let's start with Tramp. A few months ago I was called to visit Tramp in his home by a very distraught human mom. The family was trying to make the decision whether it was time for Tramp to be put to sleep, or not. When I arrived Tramp and his brother Truman, both Labradoodles were sitting on the sidewalk side by side with a lady, who was their caretaker. As I got out of the car, and began walking towards him, Tramp suddenly lifted his head and gazed directly at me... and I could Feel in my body and Heart that no way was this fellow ready to leave his body; he had work to do! I honor this.

When I came to be beside Tramp he was helped up off the ground to standing position by his friend and helper. He was basically not able to walk, could stand for a short while, but had essentially lost hind end support and movement. Still I could Feel deeply he did not want to go yet. And I expressed this to all the folks who had gathered around by now. There were quite a few people honoring Tramp today.

Inside the house there were at least 8 people and we all sat in a circle in the living room. Tramp and Truman wanted to stay outside with their human companion for awhile. This was fine with me as I could Feel Tramp in my Heart and my body clearly. The one thing that was outstanding to me in all of this was how deeply I already "knew" these humans and Tramp and Truman. How many times had we all been together before? There was no question that I was among dear friends from many journeys here and in other realms.

Each person was very deeply connected to Tramp. There were the daughter, the son, the son's girlfriend, the mom's brother and sister, mom, dad and a girl from the neighborhood who really loved Tramp. It was an amazing experience for me, and at one point one of the people said (and this was repeated several times throughout the session) how, because of Tramp, all of them had come together, had been pulled together in deeper love of one another because of this being in the Sacred Vessel of Dog.

The extent of surgeries, of nearly dying (twice), of acute onsets, of chronic diseases, of issues since puppyhood (Tramp was 8 now)....
And it is enough for me to say it was overwhelming for me to hear and feel it all. The family was essentially in shock from years of trying to help Tramp stay in his body; and Tramp was in deep bodily pain and weakness and weariness from years of helping these humans; of "doing his job" that he Contracted for with this family. All free will, and yet....
All the veterinarians who knew Tramp loved him and doted on him.

About half way through the long and painful telling of Tramp's story he was brought into the room from outside, and he and his brother Truman laid down in the middle of the circle, butt to butt. After they were settled and they had received loving offering of water, the discussion continued. I made a point of asking each person, now 9 people, how they felt about Tramp, what had gone on with him, what was now going on with him, what each felt would be the most Loving gestures to him now. Each being was so unique in his/her relationship to him. Each one was so deeply in gratitude for him. I was blown away! For I had never experienced a group of people, family and neighbors, so devoted to an animal in this way. A profound lesson for me, who had come from a very different family and human relationships to animals. A very deep Healing went on in me in that room!

There was such uncertainty as to what "to do" for Tramp on the part of the humans, a big part of this was their own suffering that they were projecting onto him. I explained to them that unlike humans with their ego mind, the animals are not attached to a sense of "ego-I" nor to appearances and right and wrong and judgments about how to do something; rather they live in the emotional body and the physical body, are not attached to what happens to their body as an identity with the "ego-I" as humans tend to be, until we can evolve a sense that we are not the ego. There are of course the instinctive mechanisms that keep the body alive, that help the organism survive as a separate unit at any cost... but there is not the ego mind's need for "how things should/ought to be." There is a deep surrender in animals, to whatever needs to be done; their ego identity lies in "getting the job done" at any cost. They literally do not care about what happens to their bodies, their emotional fields, just so the job gets done! One aspect of this "job getting done" is that I, Betsy Shoh Nah Hah Lieh, hears many a time from the animals, "Do not be too hard on my people!"

So what was needed from my own perspective was that the humans clarify their own relationship to all that had gone on with Tramp, was going on now, and what might be in future. How much more caretaking were they able to continue, did they want to do more caretaking? In view of Tramp's physical disability,... and too, there was cancer now, fairly advanced according to Tramp himself. And yet, it was obvious this dog Being was in no way ready to be euthanized. He just was not done.

Thus we arrived at a crucial point that I've helped animals and their people many times now: how much more is the human able to take? How much more does the human want to do? How much more can the human do without doing physical &/or emotional damage to the self? How much is the human invested in the suffering of the animal (conscious and unconscious)? How much is the human NOT taking care of the human, in exactly the same manner that the animal, in order to serve is NOT taking care of the animal? One mirroring the other in the tendencies of overserving at one's own expense. There is no self Love in any of this. And where is the need to be egoically loving in order to feel better about the self in all this - to assuage the egoic guilt of "never can do enough?" To make it so the human can, literally, sleep at night without beating on the self.

It is true that the animals will lie awake at night when the human is suffering so much, it is their job they believe, and by Contract, to download the human to help the human see what they are up to; how the human is creating out of a deep lack of self Love all this suffering the human is experiencing. As I've said, the animals do not care what happens to them in all this service to us. And I always ask the people how they feel about this (not think, but feel), that the animals just do not care how much they have to take on just so the human is happy, is helped the best the animal can help. I have had only one human in thousands who actually replied, "Well, I really don't care, just so I get better in all this... I am suffering so much, it really does not matter to me whether my animal is or not." This human really meant this, she was sick unto death of suffering and had nothing left over for someone else's suffering, even if that someone was helping her.

I will be honest and say that at that time (this was many years ago) I was shocked by this woman's seeming unfeeling selfishness. But I am like the vast majority of "animal people" who have the tendency to "put their animals first;" which on the inside, deep inside the ego is a way to keep on suffering... And oh!, I did not want in any way shape or form to accept this when I first hacked onto it!

Most people will say No! they do not want their animal to continue downloading their stuff at the animal's expense; and then comes how to help with all this. How to help the animal stop downloading (see Prayer the Animals gave me), and how to help the human become more conscious of what is being downloaded from them by the animal. To do this latter requires that the human turn first to self Loving Gestures and honestly and without judgment on the self, feeling how they really feel as best they are able; to turn to the Love That Is Prior to their suffering here, and realizing HereIn lies the Healing. And then, spontaneously the animals, if they so choose, can get out from under the downloading, stop being a mirror of this suffering of the human (which if one feels, and Feels, into it has become the suffering of the animals almost literally).

In Tramp's case, what these dear friends and family decided was to allow Tramp to decide for himself when he was ready to go; or if that time came when it was just too much for the humans to care for his body, his disabilities - which now including his not knowing he was peeing or pooing, becoming unable to be mobile in the back end, or the pain just became too much for the humans to witness anymore, they would call the in-home veterinarian they loved and have him helped in this way.

It has come in again to mention the New Animals, the New Children. These New Beings are coming into the Earth realm Feeling the Love that

PreExists the feeling of ego separation – bringing It in and Radiating It so we can All Feel this again! There are wonderful books and online resources on this available. The young people in Tramp's family are New Children, and although they of course still have ego, their Feeling Beyond ego was apparent in their Heart Feeling concern about the feelings that Tramp might be experiencing and his Spiritual welfare, rather than the "how can we fix this problem" of all but one of the older people in the room. I expressed to the family that Tramp could come back whenever they wanted him to; his Soul could come back in a new vessel more in alignment with the New Animals, Feeling the Love and the self Love and while being with his people again, he need not do the downloading that had been such a heavy work for him this time around. The animals we love, and who "leave us" can come back at any time, we just need ask, and Feel in our Hearts when the time is right.

# MoonBoy & Tramp Part 2

When I returned home from the visit with Tramp's family and friends, I was in a very joyful space. Here were humans who loved this Tramp, this being in Dog Vessel, so much... This joy carried deep into the night for me, and my meditation was deep and steady.

The next day was a beautiful sunny brilliant day with all my critters wanting to go out! So of course I let them go. We live in the wilderness and all are safe to go out whenever they like. MoonBoy, who is in his fourth life in Sacred Vessel as Cat with me went out in the mid-afternoon. He usually comes back by the next morning, or at least by two days later. There is a lot to explore here! It has been very interesting to me that since this truly Divine October weather we are having it is like no one "lives here" anymore... by this I mean that it Feels like the creatures are "gone"... where, I do not know, but it Feels in my bodyHeart as though they are visiting Home, or perhaps their Families of Light on the space ships or in the InterGalactic Libraries of Light, or ... the other levels ... who knows!? Whatever, the feeling (note the little "f" here) of the bodies of my animal friends being "absent" or "in latency" was strong. I was fine with it all.

MoonBoy has not returned and it has been 5 days and 5 nights now. Jewell, his mother a soft grey very powerful serene Being has been sleeping near me the last three nights. Tonight I decide to deal with my anxiety, my loneliness, my missing him, my fear something awful has happened to him, what, what, what...? My ego is really up! My ego mind's need to know is really up! God Bless Jewell, who has been with me in 7 bodies now, coming and going since my being a very small child to help me be here, to survive and evolve.

I begin to do my meditation and my Prayer, my connection to What Lives Me, I turn to this. I ask that every Breath I Breathe Love into every cell of my body, every aspect of my Being, my entire Essence; and that I Receive this Love and that everything that is not Love First be released back to God,... I surrender as best I am able All to the Beloved, I Surrender All... Whooooosh the Breath is Breathed Out, Released, ... I am crying hard by now, and I can feel I cannot any longer run away from the pain and fear I am feeling, that has just been gripping me and gripping me for the last 2 days and nights... In spite of the clenched chest around my Heart I Breathe In I Breathe Out I Receive I Surrender I Pray for help from Michael, and I remember and Feel how it is not that Michael did not feel the pain, but that He Loves, that he Chooses to Be Love First no matter how deep the pain. How Michael in every moment Chooses to Feel the Love Prior To this pain, this fear, this need to know gnawing away at my ego self.

I begin to physically feel my Heart expanding with the pain, the deep pain not only of me, my ego, my pain for Mooney, but also for all of Earth, the Animals, the Beings everywhere who are trapped in this choice of the egoic mechanisms, who are feeling separate even as I feel separate. I feel the compassion for them, for me. And then, I Feel Compassion, the Heart Opening and Feeling and taking IN ALL THE LOVE Into this pain, I allow this Love to penetrate the pain, the fear, the need to know, I ALLOW myself to Receive the Love, the self Love. And all the pain dissolves in this Love, this Truth, this All There Is, Love, self Love.

And I fall asleep in peace for the first time in many nights, Jewell purring beside me, gently pressed to my side.

When I awaken the next morning, I am feeling again the pain and the fear, but I am also Feeling the deep Breath and Openess of my Heart to "WhatEver"... that I am truly Surrendered to whatever it is that MoonBoy has decided to do. For he is a Divine free will being, even as I. What he is choosing to do I need to Trust.

And I must be very honest and report here that even though MoonBoy had been communicating with me about one time per day up until this morning I had been antsey and fear filled as to his whereabouts. For the last three days leading up to this morning, day 6 and counting! Ego counting! This little bugger does not stop until it is fully dissolved in the Love... someday, someday... it WILL Happen!... For three days leading up to this one, MoonBoy had told me as follows: "I'm Ok mom, don't worry." Next day, "I'm still here. I've not left the Planet." and Next day, "I'll be back mom.".... and inspite of clearly feeling/Feeling in my Heart and body his voice and impressions I have also been deeply in my egoic fear as to his welfare and what could have happened to him. Ahhhh, how that masochistic little ego, with its sadistic ego mind, loves to suffer, to create suffering!!! I am fully aware of all this, I am learning more and more to be a "witness" to this behavior, disengaging with Love from these tendencies of my ego/super ego... learning, learning... As they say, "It's Over when its Over!"...

In over 30 years I've had over 500 kitties, 25 doggies and thousand wildlife that I have cared for and given home to. Over and over of course these beings leave their bodies, die, transition,... and as the years have passed I am still like it is all the first time for me! I have never really gotten used to it all. It is this, that I am in a dual state: feeling the leaving of this being in a body from me in a body here, being left behind by this being AND Feeling the profound Transformation that occurs when the Soul is setting Free, moving out of the body, leaving the body behind... AND, this is the very interesting part, depending on the evolution of the Soul and the body created by this Soul and the Sacred Body Factories and God, the relationship of the vessel to being left behind by the Soul is very unique. I have a very dear friend who literally Feels and feels the body and the Soul during these transitions by the animals, how the body in one case felt totally bereft when the Soul left, like "all the lights went out." And in another case how the body remained filled with Light, even after the Soul had moved on. And then, there is where does the Soul go when it leaves the body? And what Really happens to the body, this Divine Sacred Vessel after "death?" There is so much we do not "know;" but there is so very much that we can, if we want to learn and Attend, to Choose, FEEL at transition of the perceived "other."

And so, I awoke on day 6 of MoonBoy being gone, "gone" ... and I went as is my habit to my computer to check on email. There, the first one and only one from Tramp's caretaker: "Tramp passed on this morning." I was stunned. My ego took a big hit with this, and yet I could also simultaneously Feel how All Is Fine. This dual existence right now, Feeling the Love That Is that orchestrates when we Allow and Surrender, and that egoic resistance to all of this, to wanting to be in control or something "bad" will, has, happened... Overall I was egoically concerned that he had been put to sleep by the family as they just could not do anymore, take anymore. Why I was so concerned in this manner just flushed up from my unconscious, and certainly was not a Loving relationship to what was transpiring. (I observe this...)

I went to the phone and called the mother right away, and she said "Yes, I found him at 8am this morning, he had passed away in the night on his own." What a profound Gift! In spite of the grief and that Tramp would be deeply missed, I could feel how relieved the mother was that it had happened this way. And interestingly, the father was out of town on business, the daughter out of town for four days (Tramp was closest to this daughter), the son and all the others were in their own homes. Mom had been all alone with Tramp on that night and today. She explained that she had sat down beside Tramp the night before and told him how much she loved him, and told him stories of his puppyhood, and how it was OK whatever he wanted to do, the family would be there for him. And then...

When I hung up I was crying, both for joy and the Feeling of Compassion for this beautiful family. I decided it was time to check on my own furrie family and so I went to the door and opened it. And there came MoonBoy running up to the door, tail raised, meowing joyfully, happy just as though he had been gone for an hour into this SunLight of God. Needless to say I about (egoically) had a heart attack; but I was also Feeling in my Healing Heart how Divinely OK ALL IS!!

I called Tramp's mom back to tell her my story, how Moon had disappeared the day after I was at their home, and how he now shows up within a minute after my hanging up the phone after her sharing with me on Tramp's departure. Truly Wondrous Are The Ways Of The Beloved!

After all, it was completely out of my (ego's) hands. It always is; in fact we control nothing here. But for the Divine Breath and Being we would not even be here having this egoic and Healing exploration! All I can do is Surrender, and Trust, and when that resistance arises (which is 100% the natural state of the ego, super ego... it's got a job to do!); I need to turn to the Love That Is, Always, in every moment Turn to this Love that is pouring into this Planet, this Universe and all the Universes Forever Infinite Love. Michael Innocence once said, "In every moment, even though I am Free and Feeling the Prior State, the Love, in every moment I, too, must Surrender All to the Beloved."

MoonBoy slept for awhile, maybe an hour or so, and then got up, wanting to go outside again on this Beautiful Day of Brilliant Light. I was feeling OK with this, and as he sat on the porch looking around, I said to him with my Heart Overflowing, "I Love You, I will miss you, please be careful!"... He turned around and looked at me, and came back into the house, and slept for 24 hours! I am still working on this one! Oh, the unconscious ego and its needs, how it will erupt forth and suddenly be expressing, over riding the Love in My Heart! I am Truly still a work in progress!... And One Day... One Day...

He is out there now, in the Vastness of His Heart, Held in the Love That Is. Always. We All Are. Always.

God Bless Tramp God Bless MoonBoy God Bless All the Humans All the Animals All the Life We Are That Lives Us All Deepest Gratitude on this Day Earth Day LOVE

# What am I expecting from my animal?...

hat am I expecting from my animal? Who is this being to me? There is the conscious reply to this, and there is the unconscious relationship to this question. The conscious relationship we have with our animal friends rides on a deep subterranean unconsciousness that is always in flux. This flux is part of the feedback loop between my ego's needs and how they are being fed, or "met."

When I go back to my childhood I remember so vividly my relationship to the animals in my life, how curious I was about them, how they interacted in various ways with me, with Nature, with each other; how nurturing they were for me. In this latter case they were "filling me up" where I felt empty relative to humans' filling my needs. The outstanding feeling I always had was I was never being judged by my animals, never questioned, always accepted for who I was in that moment with them, and in fact this carried over into even when we were not together physically. I could feel their love for me no matter where I was. This was not true for any of the humans at this point in my existence here.

This feeling of complete acceptance and love for me by the animals over all these years – I am now 70 – has never changed. Even though the lessons have been tough and the death, dying, transition and transformation of the many animals has occurred, I can still feel their love through all of it. The human love story has been a much rockier road, with many more bumps and lumps, and surprises too!

I need to start this part of the story backwards, from where I am now, in this moment, which is Yearning with all my Heart To Be Love First, no matter what. That's important, the No Matter What part... the ego in every way lives conditionally, "if/then," "who how where when why," all of these last five being conditional experiencial relationships to myself and others and events. But, to Be Love First, No Matter What is saying in big bold Letters that Love IS and is UN-conditional. That no matter what the event, who the person or animal, how painful the experience, I Choose To Be Love, To Be Loving. I Choose to Live in this Unconditional relationship to everything that arises here. Michael said, and I repeat it here again, "Just because it is karma does not mean it is Spiritually appropriate." This implies free will, Choice,...which will I choose?

When I judge myself, no matter how tiny that judgment may be or feel, I am being in a conditional relationship to myself, to my ego. When I Love myself, I am Choosing to be in an Unconditional Loving relationship to myself. And, whether I am conscious of it or not, when I am judging myself I am choosing to be unLoving to myself. It is a choice, albeit, an unconscious choice in certain instances.

The effect of this unLoving choice on my animals is what all this preamble has been leading up to; my judgments upon my self directly impact my animals at many levels - emotionally, physically, mentally, Spiritually. The animals are my energetic mirror, and especially, as I've stated before, they are profoundly my mirror of my unconscious patterns and tendencies that are making me not happy Happy. And when I am not Happy I am not Being Me, but rather I am being the unHealed egoic me. The True Me is Truly Loving. No Matter What.

One of the biggest confusions that arises here is around being Relationally Loving No Matter What. To be Loving does not mean I allow myself to be abused, mistreated, pushed around, and so on; it does mean I Choose to be Loving to myself First, Feeling the Love of God Living Me, and I Relate from this Space and Feeling. I Choose to not relate from my egoic tendencies as best I am able (it is not about perfection, is is an exploration here). This last is something that needs to be learned (perhaps Re-learned?), practiced, Attended to in every moment and, ultimately, arises spontaneously from the Love That Lives Us All. It is not like I am "making it happen;" we could say I am in these Moments <u>Gifted</u> with the appropriate Relational response with whomever or whatever I am in Relation to. It definitely does not come from the ego mind, which notoriously thrives on being unLoving and unLoved. This is part of its job description. Sad, but true.

A keynote to Loving and Being Love First is that I am not changed by circumstances that arise here. I am not "reactive" to whatever is happening to me or around me. My ego may be being "reactive," but I Am not. To Be Love is to Be Un-changed by anything, anyone, any event that arises in our phenomenological Universe. This takes disciplined and truly committed practice to arrive in this State, but for me is worth every moment of dedication.

And most importantly for all of our animal friends, it Helps them to Heal too, if they desire to Heal, for it is their own free will Choice just as it is mine. They no longer have to mirror back all my unconscious conditional reactive unLoving stuff, but rather get to feel (and Feel when the time is right) and mirror back all the Loving! To Feel all the Loving! Isn't this a Great Thing!? Yes, and the animals have to want this too. They are egoically (karmically) bound by Contracts and free will agreements with us, with Earth, with each other all along the paths to Freedom from the egoic bondage here. It is what they signed on for, and we did too. What a Trip this Is!

So my relationship to myself, to others, I need to ask : Is it UN-conditional? Am I pretty much surrendered to whatever the Universe has in store for me, or am I asking for something? Am I being disappointed when something doesn't turn out the way I (my ego) wants? Am I feeling like I'm not getting what I deserve from someone, some event here? Constantly seeking and seeking and seeking to get my needs met from another being? Am I being reactive in ways that demonstrate right now, here in front of myself, how not Loving I am? How I am judging others for not giving me what I want, need, feel I deserve? Am I blaming mom and dad and brother and sister and the rest of this extended Planetary Human Family for not doing what I want!? What I need!!? NOW!!?? Waaaaah!! Waaaaaaaaahhh!! Time for a Tantrum!!! I can feel it coming on!!!!!

Whew! When will this all be "over?" That is really easy to answer: When I turn to the Love I Am and not keep catering to my ego and all its really infantile tendencies and demands. So, let's have a Party and All Grow Up! How? Many Many Many pathways to this One: looking into the Heart of your dear animal is for sure one of them. Feeling in your own Heart when you are with another human, is this human a Feeling human, or is this human into power and domination, or its flipside submission and masochism? Vigilance with regard to who you choose to be with, relate to, is critical: LOVING Vigilance, not judging, not based in fear, not based in the energies of the famous triad.

What Gifts abound here as teachings... this whole Planet, this whole Universe that resonates our feelings, and our Feelings, back and forth, shared and mutually Lived. If we could but stand in our feelings long enough to gaze into these resonating mirrors within and "without"... to stand and allow ourselves to feel how we feel : embrace and Love Thru our fear of "something is wrong with me" "I am a bad person" "I must be a bad person because I am so sick all the time" "I don't feel I really deserve happiness" and yatta yatta yatta... NONE OF THIS yatta yatta IS REAL! It is just the ego mind yakking away. That's its job! Let it yak! We get to Choose to Be Whatever It IS that we ARE. In alignment with the Divine, all the time, in every moment. Thank You God!

# Trauma as a "set up" for Waking Up

Yesterday I received a call from a family in which the dog had bitten the lady's hand, very hard, very painfully. These people really care deeply about this dog and in past this dog has been a very "Noble" animal. Over the past few months there have been a couple of nipping issues, one with a small girl when she was playing with the dog. All incidents have occurred around food. In the last months, too, the dog has been growling when food is being prepared, and when it is set down on the floor for him. The ladies of the house have done their best to firmly explain to the dog there is to be no growling. Yesterday he was growling, and as the lady explained, normally he will stop when asked to stop growling, and having in past been fed immediately when the growling ceases, the same techniques and requests were made... in this case however, and the lady says she completely cannot figure out what happened, how it happened, how one minute she was firmly asking the dog to stop growling and then, bang!, somehow her left hand was in the dog's mouth, she was dragged down and the dog began to "chew" on her hand.

It took three times of talking very strongly while in pain and shock telling the dog to let go before the dog "heard" and responded and let go, sat back, with a look on his face of "what just happened?" The dog did not move or do any further actions aggressively, not even to ask for the food, which had yet to be placed on the floor for him. I asked this lady to tell me in detail exactly what had happened, and as she explained, everything was exactly the same, except this time, in accordance with a training DVD she had been studying, when the dog would not stop growling upon her asking him to, she lightly "tapped" the dog on the foot/thigh area to "get his attention," to "make him pay attention." Then this lady remembers nothing until she became aware that her left hand was in the dog's mouth.

The blanking-out by this lady is, to me, very significant; and the other significant thing to me is that the dog, when he finally responded to "stop biting me!" was as though he "came back" and that he too did not "remember" exactly what had happened, how it had all come about. For me there are several explanations that my ego mind is diligently seeking to explain this behavior; the keynote of rabies is "unprovoked aggression" of which, according to Richard Pitcairn, DVM and Martin Goldstein, DVM, there is an epidemic. It is called the "Rage Syndrome" and develops in dogs vaccinated with the rabies vaccine. Brain tumors also have this "clicking on/clicking off" with no memory of what just happened. And thirdly, something from the other levels "stepped in and created a Spiritual, or not so Spiritual, set up." This latter I have experienced in my own life hundreds of times, and in clients and their animals (both the humans and their animal friends) many hundreds of times.

These "going unconscious" moments, where we will be doing something, going along and then bang! We are somewhere else and cannot remember where we have just been, what just happened, are very common. One of the major ones is when we are driving the car and "zone out" and have actually sometimes passed our exit without being conscious, or aware until we are beyond it; or we go through what can be called "brain farts" where we suddenly lose awareness of what we just said, did, where we are, etc.

How these latter happen can be in several ways: an altzheimer type brain impairment, a brain injury where areas once connected in the brain are no longer in communication (includes tumors, growths, strokes, degenerative neurological processes), and many times by entities who have come to involve themselves in the beings' energy fields. Many of these entities are not so nice, and can, by tying into the unconscious tendencies of the individual or group they visit, create a lot of traumatic change that feels to the beings inhabited as though we are "out of control" "can't remember" "feel driven to do...", and some actually saying, "I did NOT do that!" certain that it was not their own free will choice in that instance. And so on... Also here needs to be mentioned the well documented effects of the Earth Changes energies with their amped up and Love Filled frequencies... we could say the ego mind is dissolving in Love, in the Light of the Beloved, which can certainly create interesting and often intense mental and emotional and bodily physical changes.

Again, it is critical to remember that this is a free will Universe, a free will ego field we inhabit; and I always remember Angel the kittie and her wonderful statement to us that night while she sat atop the stairwell post: "You cannot have in your awareness that which you are not!" That many of these energies, entities, beings tie into the unconscious and remain "hidden" from "view," i.e., from our conscious mind, is part of the exploration here. And in fact, often these entities, though helping to create apparent life negative scenarios, may have incorporated into their activities very Positive Opportunities if we would but Pay Attention, study what "sets us off," ATTEND to our feelings in the moment and honor them... i.e., get out of the ego mind and into the emotional body aspects of the self and become responsible for our feelings more consistently and consciously. And Meditate.

Many of these entities are very benevolent, can be called "guides" or Families of Light, or Angels, or any of hundreds if not thousands of energetically beneficial offerings to us, to our Opening to the Love We Are. What matters, and this is always true no matter what, is: What is my Relationship to this entity? What is my Relationship to myself, to My Self, and how does being in different relationship alter these entities and their "lessons" - i.e., the "set up" that from our Higher Self, our Soul, or Beyond, we are actually ASKING to have occur, and impact our lives so we Wake Up! Become Conscious of what our unconsciousness is attracting to itself. What kinds of energies are being attracted to the unconscious that is running our lives in negative ways can be a major focal point for visitations. And again I will say, we are not victims, we are creating our reality. We might express it thus: we are in every moment creating our own unique universe. The harmonically resonating nature of this ego field, this Universe, will draw to us Exactly what we are "asking for"... unconsciously and/or consciously.

So, as far as this dear dog, this being who is as he has said to me, "Just doing my job"... how much more Loving would it be that both the human and the dog become more conscious of what they are drawing to themselves in their unconsciousness - these unLoving energies that can appear as imbalances, diseases, as traumas, as events of great drama and despair. Why continue to do it this way when we can be in Relationship Lovingly to the self as best we are able; asking that ONLY those energies that are Loving and in Loving Alignment for the Highest Good be allowed into our field, into our animal's field. The animals will do anything to help their humans evolve … egoically evolve, and when the time is right, Spiritually evolve. This dog, we could say, "went unconscious" or blanked out because he had to do a job he loathed doing, in order to wake his human up. This is one of possibly several interpretation of this event.

One good measure of what might have happened is where the human, in this case the lady, was emotionally and mentally and physically before, during, and after the event. Number one, she never stopped loving the dog, even though she felt disappointment and as she said, "I really took it personally! It really hurt!" But she was never afraid of the dog, she was more shocked that he would ever do such a thing to her as she loves him so much! And then, she went on, (she "escalated here") she started yelling, "What's wrong with me? Why does this stuff always happen to me!? Why am I always getting abused even when I love someone?! I am a total fuckup!!" At which point I said as quietly as I could for I could feel how charged this energy was, - "There, do you see where you suddenly turned on yourself with your ego mind and began to judge yourself? Where did this come from?"

And she became very quiet, and she said she did not know, she could not "find it"… it was not consciously available to her. These unconscious aspects of her (and of all our) sado-masochistic infantile ego are part of the mechanism of the ego, and are NOT the true Self. They are a conditioned bag of emotional reactivities, with the ego mind development to try and keep them under control. IT IS NOT WHO WE ARE. We are not this ego, this mechanism for exploring in the ego field - what it feels like to not feel Love, to not feel Loved.

And as long as these egoic self damaging energies are present, we attract the same energies to the self. And when the time comes to "Wake Up," (and this is something between the Soul and God, it is unique and must be honored by each being, by all,) we will have the "Lessons" the "Set Ups" and what are termed "Spiritual Crises." These Crises will occur more and more frequently and can become extremely intense as we are Waking Up. But we are calling to these energies that perpetuate the Crises in order to learn to Love the self, to Feel Love and Be Love No Matter What. (Please see Karen Bishop's book, Bibliography)

Those animals who have the Soul Contracts with us, to help us Wake Up, will do anything to help us. They do not care if they die, if they are beat, if they are pushed away from us and placed somewhere else... just so the "Job Gets Done!" The animals who are doing these jobs, and in my experience on Earth in these amazing times, is, as I've indicated before, around 85% still doing it this way, are in a lot of emotional pain and suffering also; their relationship to this however is very different from the human's which is all tied up in the "self image" of the "ego-I" which is basically ruled by the ego mind, very unLovingly.

# Rude awakening or Loving, Conscious Awakening?

uilt into our systems here in this Universe is the tendency that when there is resistance against something, there is an increase in the force of impact; this impact can be viewed in living beings as trauma. The egoic resistance to Receiving Love creates in the human and the animal, as well as other beings in this ego field, a greater likelihood of experiencing trauma. Because the egoic mechanism is programmed to not be able to Receive Love, feels cut off from Love, and is seeking little love from other egos, it is constantly experiencing traumatic events on the emotional level especially, although we have all experienced physical and mental traumas too. (Please see Jung, von Franz studies of the Self, in contrast to the individuating ego; also in Michael Innocence's papers, yet unpublished)

One of the primary teachings when in Spiritual Practice and it has become a common mantra we all know, "Go with the flow." Other such sayings include the metaphor of how the grass bending before the wind does not break – i.e., the grass is putting up little resistance to the force of the wind impacting each of its blades and hence its cellular and molecular and atomic structures, thus sustaining little or no "damage." Imagine a world with no resistance, how does this feel to you? What is it we are actually in resistance to? Where there are "survival" instincts, or issues, or tendencies, we are assuming there is something we are fighting against in order to stay alive, or be here, or keep as the saying goes, "body and Soul together." To fight against is to have resistance to perceived threat to one's welfare, to one's being, to one's integrity, to one's physical survival. This is a very natural, and egoic way of being.

There is the feeling in the ego-I of "being alone against (resistance) the world," of having to find ways to succeed and overcome obstacles (perceived blocks outside the self that create resistance against which one has to fight); that nothing is of value unless it is "fought for." All of these scenarios are fundamental beliefs based in Darwinian evolutionary interpretations. And none of them are necessarily true at all. There is a way of viewing existence here as a never ending flow of Abundance that each one can Receive by being in Alignment with the flow from whence the Abundance comes. Now, if we feel and Feel into the two different ways of viewing and feeling the world; which has the greater trauma ingrained in the beliefs about life here?

Built into the physical vessel, which I truly believe is a Divine Vessel created for the given Soul for exploration in the ego field are the necessary energetic components. It is created in the Sacred Body Factories by millions of beings who have done such things for trillions of years. We are, each one, of I cannot even guess how many experiments in "what happens" when certain free will choices are made as foundations for certain explorations in all the Universes available for explorations. And many explorations are done without the use of a physical, high density Sacred Vessel; but Vessels of Light, of very high frequencies...

Who or what are the beings who have helped create the Sacred Vessels? There are many many "myths and legends" about the visitations here, and elsewhere; about the "interventions" and biogenetically engineered beings who inhabit, and have inhabited, our Earth: we humans, the animals, plants, ... and?.... how many other lifeforms have come here, are here now? (please see Sitchin and Wingmakers in Bibliography, plus many online resources)

In our case there is built into our vessels a deep identification with the bodymindemotions that is so human, where the ego identity of the human is all wrapped up in how the body appears, how the being fits in the group, how the being is succeeding against the odds, how the being is supportive/nonsupportive of others, how "selfish" one is and the interesting development of judgment around these issues, and many more. There is such a need in the ego-I for acceptance by others because it cannot Love itself, and cannot Receive Love; it is by its very creation, energetically in resistance to this. So the seeking of little love in order to feel safe, in order to feel wanted, in order to feel good about the ego-I, has developed here in this realm with unimaginable consequences that we are all living today.

There is, however, also built into the Sacred Vessel, that Yearning for Home, i.e., that Yearning to Feel Love again. There are energetic structures built into the pineal gland as well as into other parts of the Sacred Vessel. There is the ability within each animal and each human to place the Attention on the energy flow, the Love, but each being has to want this, and has to Choose to place Attention upon this in every moment. Then evolution moves away from strict Darwinian survival issues and moves into what is called Spiritual Evolution with the ability to relax within the Sacred Vessel and to yield and "give over" without becoming so terrified and feeling so vulnerably unsafe and "submissive" that are built into the ego mechanisms when these activities are engaged in. There IS a way to live here while still in the body that is "slowed down and Feeling" that is non-resistant to events, while Feeling completely safe. But it requires Feeling and Believing that this is True, and can become a way of Life here, now, in every moment. (I am truly tempted to express here that the Divine Self of C.G. Jung which resides in the collective unconscious is like the Resonating Face or Being "at the bottom of the world" that is in harmonic Resonance with the Beloved, with God; A Mirror for the Beloved, for the Divinity with which we are Gifted, in every moment, in our dreams, in our visions this Divine Self, which is not human, can help Guide us Home to God. "As Above, So Below." The clarity of the Light shining down down into the depths of the world, the Lake, already at Home within our own Being if we will but Pay Attention!)

How many Meditators do you know? How many martial artists? How many friends do you have that just seem "happy all the time" no matter what is going on here? How many animals have you met or have you had as companions in this life who are just tail-wagging smiley ones? No matter what situation they are in? And yet, who are also completely competent to take care of themselves no matter what arises? And when you observe these beings "taking care of themselves" how much lack of resistance are they demonstrating, by their State, by their Station, by their Relationship to Being, and Being Here? More of a flow and a moving with what is going on... a way of remaining within the body with little or no resistance to what is happening to it, or is perceived as possibly happening to it? This way of Being Is a tremendous lessening of trauma. This lessening of resistance is a direct

75

consequence of Trust that we will be completely supported; that those aspects of the ego that are energetically contracted away from Life, from Love will fade as they dissolve in the Love. It is a process and the amount of "time it takes" is between each Soul, each unique arising here, and God. It is never truly Loving or Helpful to "rush" this process, or to take upon oneself the assumption of "Knowing more than God" as to these Openings. There is available to each and every living being here a way to exist that is Natural, that is self Loving, that is safe and in which all the needs of the bodymindemotions are met.

It is possible to Feel and to Live in this manner, but this requires wanting this before wanting to engage in those activities and mental and emotional processes that engage survival issues rooted in the fear within the ego, that lie at the core of the ego. One way of saying this is that the facing of the fear that resides within our ego is relatively freeing; and bringing the Love into this fear and dissolving this fear in Love is completely Freeing. We do not need to continue to traumatize ourselves, and have these "rude awakenings" because of our resistances to what the Divine intends for our Souls, for our Souls as manifesting here. Every so called "negative" thing that "happens" to us can have as its higher purpose the message that we are "going in the wrong direction" and the event that is occurring to us, that feels so negative can be in fact a "wake up call" to get us onto track and into alignment with the Divine - something we Contracted for before we ever incarnated here in the ego field, at the Soul levels and beyond.

It is OK to have Loving, non traumatic wake ups! And we get to decide with our own free will that we would like to live this way. We have to make free will life choices rooted in Trusting and Feeling that Things Will Work Out, and turn away from manipulaton through fear that if we don't "do" something, something will happen that is "bad." There is, in fact, no "risk" when Loving. The song by Jimminy Cricket is how we might learn to behave... "whenever I feel afraid I hold my head erect, And whistle a happy tune so no one will suspect I'm afraid... You may be as brave As you make believe you are!" One needs to ACT AS THOUGH it is true, and whether ego wants to believe this or not, it IS True because We Are Creating It through our Feeling it to be true. Creating it through the shifts in our own energy bodies, and in our alignments with the flow of this Love, the Divine, that is always here.

I would like to mention here the works by Michael Roads, his "Journeys Into Nature" and his "Into a Timeless Realm" specially. The most powerful Feeling that emanates from his works, in which he is with his wife and dear companion, exploring Nature, the Universe, is one of Surrender and Allowing whatever is happening to happen. There is one section of "Into A Timeless Realm" in which he is being shown by his guide the truly beautiful relationship, I will call it Relationship for it is based in Feeling Love, of the Laplanders of long ago to their animals at the time of needing food and other materials for the clan, the tribe. What happens is this: the males go and Feelingly choose the reindeer who is to become the sacrifice so the Laplander humans can eat and sustain their bodies here. The males bring this reindeer to the women, who gather round this animal and begin to sing to it. This is a very deep Heart Feeling ceremony, during which the reindeer lies down and Surrenders its Soul, its Breath, to the Universe. Then when this sacrificial Gesture on the part of the reindeer is made with complete free will, and the body has been "left behind" and is no longer "inhabited" do the Laplanders begin to utilize the body for food and other Gifts given by this being's Sacred Vessel. When I first read this in Michael Road's book I just sat and cried. Of course! This is the manner in which we can all be to our animals, to each other, to all life; it IS a matter of free will and Surrender to Relationship in each moment that creates Joy here; or contrary desolation, bereft feelings of abandonment. It need not at all be about "dying," and the unconscious, unLoving utilization of others' vessels; it can occur in every moment, this Loving of each other, Serving of each other. It is a matter of whether we want to be Love First and move from this Space, or stay stuck in our egoic resistance and all it creates here so unLovingly. I recall Michael telling me something very interesting: "You could be eating a MacDonald's hamburger, and if you are in appropriate Relationship to it, you could Open to God Fully in that Moment."

A few days ago, along these same lines, a friend sent to me online a wonderful video of the "Weeping Camel" which was the true present day event occurring in a Nomadic Mongolian tribe here on Earth. This mother camel would not accept her newborn, and so the tribe asked a Shaman, in this case female, to come and to sing to the mother to help this mother camel overcome her resistance to her baby and the baby's need to find nurturance from the mother. The film is exquisite and again, the free will of the mother camel with regard to Surrendering to the Love that flowed in the Song, the Song of this Shaman whose Heart is Open to the Universe, to Love That Lives Her... the newborn was soon feeding! Please see the bibliography for Michael Road's works cited as well as the webpage for this video. More and more on the internet are the stories and photo series of humans with animals, loving animals, turning to the spaces of service and not dominance, to the Spaces of Loving Service from the free will. The animals are learning to Receive this Love, and are Surrendering to the Receiving of Love, as we all must one day.

And of course the other side is that trauma is self-created by our beliefs in our separation from the Love We Are. We are, you could say, "victims" of our own beliefs: because we hold onto these resonating bands of energetic fear that lie in the ego field and strum and strum them over and over, calling out to the trauma to "come and get me!" It is actually rather absurd how we are treating ourselves; and how the animals are treating themselves in order to serve us. None of it is necessary at all. But we CHOOSE. We humans choose and the animals choose too. Earth is in the process of giving up all this trauma and drama; Earth Changes are a profound opportunity to move on "up" the frequencies out of the dark egoic formats and into the Love We Are Already. What is holding me back? Something Michael has said that always makes me smile or laugh out loud: "DOUBT THE DOUBT!"

# Cults and their effects on our animal friends

A few years ago a woman contacted me concerning her Spiritual practice and what had been, several years earlier, asked of her by her teacher. This lady had never really gotten over the trauma of what she had done at the behest of this teacher, feeling at the time she should follow what the teacher told her to do unquestioningly. Over many years this woman had been involved in stray rescue work and had kept many of the animals she had "saved" during this time. She worked with several rescue, placement and foster homes for animals in the area where she lived and worked.

Her teacher had, a few years before she contacted me, told her she needed to "get rid of" some of her animals; that having so many animals was interfering with her Spiritual practice and growth. This woman, because she really believed in her teacher did as she was told. There was, as she was describing it to me, a deep sense that there was no room for discussion with this teacher, that the teacher had absolutely no doubt about the correctness of the action she was asking this practitioner to carry out. This immediately set my senses, intuitive, bodily, emotionally, on alert.

What this teacher in fact wanted this lady to do was to kill those animals that were creating an "excess" of numbers and hence were interfering with this lady's Spiritual practice. Which animals exactly to do away with was not made clear, however, by this teacher to this lady. It was left up to the lady to decide which to get rid of. One of the issues about having so many animals, according to the teacher, was the amount of money that this lady spent every month feeding and caretaking her animal friends. She did as she was told and killed quite a few of her animals. It created in her, she told me, a horrible conviction that she had done something really wrong, and yet how could it be wrong when she was also sure her teacher was "right, in fact was always right" and everyone in her group was sure the teacher was "always right?" We will now term this group "cult" because of the energies that were being generated within the group by this teacher and by those who submitted to this teacher's beliefs and practices.

One thing I truly have gratitude for in this life is my mentor and friend Michael Innocence. His teaching was clear on many points around Spiritual Practice, Spiritual Evolution, the ego patterns and tendencies, self Love and what was required of the Spiritual practitioner to Become Loving and Be Love First. He was also very clear on what constituted cult practices. He would say unequivocally that each being here is Unique and that the Uniqueness of the being needed to be honored and nurtured by the teacher, by the guide in this being's life who professed to be Spiritual guide. Where there was no room for discussion or differing opinions or ways of being and manifesting, but rather the sense of enforced "sameness" or "cloning" of beings with whom the teacher was in contact, would be termed a cult.

Michael would also say that because of egoic reactivity, which are tendencies of every being in our ego field, that to be able to discern between an egoic individual who is expressing reactively and what constitutes Unique Expression is critical. I remember my own confusion around my sense of wanting to be "me" and "different" and being able to express "unhindered by anyone" my own special brand of emotions (very egoic!). I also remember my wanting to learn this critical difference between Uniqueness and being an egoic individual. The cult leader is a master (or mistress) at "saying" they are really interested in development of the Uniqueness of the being and the being's Unique Expression, BUT one discovers soon on, if that expression or way of being individual deviates even a small bit from the cult leader's expectations of the practitioner, tremendous pressure is brought to bear on the practitioner to give up their way and come into alignment energetically with the cult leader's will. This will of the cult leader is not aligned to Love but to power, the need to control others; and the cult leader is often unconscious of these unresolved issues within his/her own infantile ego.

Now, if we have a true Spiritual Teacher as Guide for a group, we will feel and Feel Love emanating from the Spiritual Teacher; but if we cannot in our Hearts and bodies Feel this Love emanating, but rather a dominating, controlling, power based energy emanating, this is not a Spiritual Teacher, but a "cult leader." A true "cloning" energetically takes place where there will be no Unique Beings within the group, but rather a group energy in which each being is subsumed, and made to submit to this group pressure, with dire consequences in terms of "acceptance" and ever "getting love" from the cult leader. The cult leader will explicity or unexplicity through with holding love from the practitioner, demand obedience. And there will be outright punishment, ostracizing, brutal bashings of the ego's emotions by the cult leader and the group. There is in fact, no matter how the cult leader may profess otherwise, no "discussion" on any of this behavior and manipulation. No matter how much the cult leader may be professing to uphold the Uniqueness of each practitioner, there is no true Loving Relationship between practitioner and cult leader. There is total dependence created, with the stuffing of emotions that is truly malignant. There is the concomitant energetic parasitism of the cult leader on the practitioners, as well as between practitioners. All of this malevolent energy sharing and feasting is basically unconscious.

For now, I want to explain how I experience how and why cults "work" and of great importance, what the impact of being in a cult has on animal friends of cult members. The primary energy of the infantile ego is to feel separate from the Love It Is, and this as written of before in this book and many other places, is part of the experiment we are all choosing to explore here in this Universal ego field. What a savvy cult leader knows is how much the ego is suffering in this feeling of being alone here, of being abandoned, of needing to feel loved (note little "I"). Cults have nothing to do with Love, but are a great way to traumatically, and often horrifically, learn about the differences between Love and egoic love. This need to feel loved that resides within the ego is built in and is part of the experiment here. The ease with which the ego is drawn into relationships where it believes it is getting little love, and deeply believes it is getting Love, are manifold. The unconsciousness of the ego and its deep patterns of feeling unworthy, unwanted, the self loathing etc etc (see Bergler's works as well as papers by Michael Innocence), are well known by psychoanalysts, psychiatrists, and psychologists worldwide. The trick is to get the ego to believe it is being loved by the cult leader while all the time this leader is manipulating the ego into really terribly self damaging practices, at the practioner's expense and the cult leader's benefit.

How is this possible? Well, because at the very core of the ego, in the depths of the unconscious of the ego, there are aspects of the unHealed self that believes it does not deserve love anyway! We all learn this by age three months if you are on the old karmic wheel here. We are in fact seeking to find ways to make sure we do NOT receive love (and Love); we seek ways that will in fact sabotage the love from another ego when it is offered to us and the Love that a True Loving Being offers to us. Those of us who have succumbed to a cult leader are those who are really in a depth of self hatred and self loathing and self unworthiness UNCONSCIOUSLY (please remember this!) that it is easy to be manipulated into doing all sorts of things to get that carrot, that "love from the teacher," that "acceptance" and that "validation" from the teacher – now called cult leader; while at the same time aligning UNCONSCIOUSLY with the deep self hatred, self loathing, that exists unconsciously in the cult leader. It is my feeling and Feeling that often the cult leader is so out of touch with the negative unconscious and how it is running the show, that the cult leader is also being duped while professing Insight, Conscious Guidance, Love... The group that "forms" and "coalesces" around the cult leader is simply mirroring the unHealed unconsciousness of the cult leader after all. (Please see Bergler's studies of the unHealed unconscious, as well as Jung's studies of the unHealed individuating self which he distinguishes from the Self; this latter he holds as of Divine Origin, which does hold the Love within itself. Jung makes a clear demarcation between the unHealed unconscious ego becoming conscious, and the Self...)

Any teacher who consciously &/or unconsciously takes advantage of the fear, the terror of not being lovable and plays on this in order to get something the teacher wants/needs is a cult leader, not a true teacher - However, in one sense they ARE in fact teaching us something in a backhanded, dark, sort of way, if we'd only Wake Up!

So, it is built in, this tendency to be taken in by those who profess love for our being while all the time we are not loving (and certainly not Loving) our self. This is a recipe for disaster; and this recipe is constantly being cooked up and we all sit down at the table and take it in like it is a normal way to exist here. I was sharing on some issues around cults and the nature of cults with a friend of mine, a psychoanalyst, who said, "I wonder just how much the human family is cult?" This is a really good question, as wherever there is suppression of the Unique Loving expression of another, or even of positive qualities of an individual, there is cult energy involved. And, remember, we choose to be in these kinds of relationships. Why? Is it truly helping the Soul to evolve? Or, is it just one more way to insure we come back and go around again and again, going through the same ole same ole in the Universe's ego field? Or...?

How was your own egoic family life? I was sharing with a friend of mine today and she was describing a family who lives across the street from her family that she really likes. The thing that impressed her the most (and we were not even remotely discussing cult energies, just happy stuff) was how the mother would go for a walk with the little boy and would just "be with" him. She would calmly and serenely "wait" for him even if he was sitting on the sidewalk for half an hour being with a stone. She was never in a "hurry" or impatient to get somewhere with him. She never seems to have something more important to do that creates the energies of his needing to hurry up and get done with whatever it is he is doing that is impeding her needs here. Wow! Happy!

How was your childhood? Did you have a mom, dad, brothers, or sisters, aunts, uncles, grandparents, like this mom? And of course, no matter what kind of family we had, no matter how we were treated, no matter how we allowed ourselves to be treated in order to get that little love from another ego!! No matter.. As Michael has written and I have sung a thousand times, "There IS ONLY Love!!" There really are no excuses.

The impact of being in a cult on the animal friends we have can be horrific because the level of mirroring of all the stuffed negative unconsciousness these animals are choosing to download truly can cause deep bodily and emotional harm in them. It does in us, why not in our animal friends? That this lady, from the beginning of this chapter, was willing to literally end the lives of several of her animal friends for fear of having withheld from her the "love" and validation from what I would call a truly irresponsibly self-serving, albeit possibly unconscious, teacher (cult leader) speaks for itself. How far are we willing to go before we Wake Up and turn to the Love that IS, that Always IS, and which will point us in directions the little ego will NOT like, nor will the ego mind like it at all! But so what? What is wrong with turning to this Love that PreExists, that is Prior To the ego, and Allowing this Love to Heal Us, and hence of course our animals? And for sure they can do this too! I have seen many of them do it! The hard part for me is this ongoing acceptance on the part of the animals' Souls to participate in this egoic downloading of unLoving, truly self damaging energies we all carry in our ego. It is time for Change!

# Death, Dying, Transition, and Ascension

I t has been my experience over the many years of my life while being with animals during their dying, or transitioning, processes that the animals are surrendered to this process. I am speaking here of the non-traumatic dying, during which the body is going through very different processes than when death is traumatic to the body. However, and I've experienced this many times with the animals, after the shock, and even during the trauma, there may be a profound letting go, even while still fully conscious... and in certain cases I have experienced, Felt, something literally "steps in" and helps "take out, take away" the Soul, the Life Energies that are being held onto by the traumatized vessel. In these latter cases I have been able to Feel in my body and my emotional field this activity on the part of Benevolent Beings coming to carry off the Transitioning energies as well as the Surrender within the vessel to this carrying off of those energies that have kept the vessel "alive" and viable here in the ego field.

There is built into the vessel, our Divine Vessel, the instinct to stay alive within the vessel, within the body, to "survive" no matter what else might be going on in the body, in the emotional and mental fields and beyond. It is part of the survival mechanism of the ego which ensures attention is paid to keeping the physical vessel viably integrated so the explorations here in the ego field can be carried out. We are not our bodies, we are not our ego; what we Really Are is something my mind cannot even begin to know or grasp. The energies that inhabit the physical vessel, and our entire essence, are beyond my comprehension; but I can Feel them, and I am aware when the time for leaving the egoic manifestation here is at hand for many animals. They will let me know in no uncertain terms that they are "ready to go" and will ask for my help during these times.

From my own experiences and as shared with me by others, there are at least two energetic processes, or "two deaths." One being the death of the physical vessel, which becomes "uninhabited" by the energies of Spirit, or Soul, or?...that have kept it "alive;" the other being the energetic "rising out of the vessel" of the Spirit, Soul, that created by its presence "life" in the vessel. This latter does not "die" in the same sense the body does, but other processes take place that have been called Transformative - we say that we "Transition," that we "Cross Over," that we "Go Home" or to "Heaven"... but the mortal coils we drop, that leaving behind of the body can be an amazing Transformation also, for the cells are conscious beings and can thus be conscious of being left behind by whatever was "living them." There are many stories to be told here, ... yes.

I will mention here something I have observed over and over in the human that does not occur in the animal leading up to as well as often during these moments of Transition: the human mind and its need to "know" and to hence "have control over outcome" comes into play even during the Transitional processes. The animal, which rests in the deeper emotional states just accepts whatever is occurring, and its Surrender to this process is astounding to me. I believe all of us have experienced over and over this process of leaving the Divine Vessel behind and moving on to "wherever" - trillions and trillions of beings here on Earth and elsewhere in the Universes.

All of us are aware of the tendency of animals to show their desire to go off on their own somewhere and leave the body. They do not show the fear we humans do around this process. I have lived in Nature for over 40 years in my life this time around, and have been gifted with many experiences of animals leaving, peacefully, in a deeply Surrendered state up to the very last breath. For some reason it is scary for many humans to go off alone into Nature and drop the body; the mind of the human, its identification with the body as being "me" creates limits to the experiences we could be having if we would choose to expand our awareness - perhaps one day to experience what Michael has called, "Dying Consciously." Feeling the profound Love We Are, the self Love We Are during this Transformation.

This is not to say that the body itself does not go through grief during the moments of Transition; it may, for it has egoically related memory banks in which reside memories of all the experiences this particular Vessel has experienced here this time around as well as memories of many lifetimes previous to this one. When these memory banks become Infused with Love, with the Love that Exists Always, all grief dissolves in the same manner as any other ego based experience. It is possible to share with our animal friends, our human friends, this Infusion of Light and Love into the Vessel at the time of Transition, if the animal, the human, and we, are truly deeply Surrendered to What Lives Us All.

I have a dear friend who has experienced whole bodily and with profoundly open emotional field and mind the Transitioning processes of three of his animals. Each being has a Unique Transition, with Unique Relationship to this perceived leaving of the Vessel by Spirit, and how the Vessel feels upon being "left behind." He and I have both discovered that at Heart if the Vessel can Feel the Love It Is and Receive this Love, this Light, there is no "being left behind" but rather a Union of the body filled with the Light and the Love with the Spirit. When there is not this Union, the Lights "literally go out" in the cells, they feel bereft, left behind, and yearn to go with Spirit but at this point in their evolution are apparently unable, or perhaps unwilling.. But when there is a Surrender and an Allowing of Feeling into the Vessel of this Love That Lives Us All, all the cells become Illuminated, Incandescently Breathing in the Love, Life of What Lives Them.

There is for those beings who are very highly evolved Spiritually a "not leaving behind" of the Sacred Vessel, but a Dissolving of this Vessel into the Light, the Love, and in this Union the Spirit and the Vessel are One and Transition of both the Vessel and the Spirit occur. "Nothing" is "left behind." There Is Only Love.

And this brings us to the Ascension process, what it means and how when we are truly Ascended, we do not "die." When we speak of Ascension, we are referring to the entire Vessel being filled with the Love while alive, here, Now. Not having to leave the body in order to Be With the Love We Are. But rather Grounding Into the Sacred Vessel in each moment the Love, Breathing the Love into each and every cell, into the entire field the entire Essence, while consciously still here, on Earth, in this Universe. If one explores this further with Feeling, one comes to realize there is no "death," not really, but rather states of consciousness, constant Transformative processes at infinite levels and in infinite realms as we choose to explore more and more Consciously. Why some of us leave the body to "Be With the Love" while others of us are choosing Being Love while here, in the body, is something that each Soul, each Unique Arising, has chosen to explore Uniquely with God.

For most of us, including myself, the body feels "temporal," will not "last," falls away, is dropped, when the work of the Soul/Spirit utilizing this Vessel is "done." This last word is loaded, yes? What does "done" mean? We could say that the Soul Feels when its time for departure is upon It; so does the body in its unique manner, and its manner of "dying" has been experienced by numberless beings over the millenia in numberless lifeforms that have inhabited our Earth and elsewhere in the Universes.

When we feel the grief we are having when another beloved leaves the body, and for sure it feels like they leave us, there is a deep connection to the bodySoul matrix that is occurring. The deep emotional chords that connect each of us to the beloved are very bound up in the egoic feelings of separation from What Lives It, what is Living All of Us, what is Living the Beloved, in the body or out of the body. And, I am, I must admit an extreme "body" person! I miss the bodies being inhabited and alive and active and HERE NOW with me. I miss the touch, the sharing that can go on only when the bodies are mutually inhabited. I miss others extremely and profoundly when they "Pass on and over" - "leaving me behind." I have a big egoic connection to everything here, I have a huge emotional and physical connection to everything here. I am impacted deeply by whoever or whatever is in my energetic field.

So I am not any different at all from any other being here who experiences loss and grief at loss. And I Thank God for my being able to, at the same time as experiencing this grief and loss, to be able to Feel the Love. I do my best to bring the Love into the unHealed energetic field, and I do my best to help my ego to Heal as to its feelings of loss and loneliness. This is a commitment and dedication I have every day now, every moment. This does NOT mean I will not feel the egoic feelings, the pain, the separation... but I do still primarily, Choose, Consciously, to bring the Love INTO all this pain, to Illuminate and Ignite the cells of my vessel so I can Feel Beyond whole bodily to the Love.

And I am, in my own case, absolutely certain in my deepest Heart that the pain will dissolve in the Love, that the ego separation will dissolve in the Love. And I will then be truly Healed.

And as I do this, especially as I am holding my Transitioning animal friend or human friend, I do my best to Breathe and to bring into myself the Love, so I am resonating with the Love which will dissolve the fear and the pain which the ego is relating to as this process of its "ending." I do my best to be Love First and I Surrender to Love and Allow Love to Flow Through me. As best I am able I Give Over to What Is Living All. And I honor to the best of my ability the Relationship of my animal friend, of my human friend, to the Love That Lives Them. I in no way "direct or guide or manipulate" the Flow, the Love That Is. When my animal friend and my human friend are ready, they will, in each their Own Unique Manner, Receive Love, and find Peace and Healing in the Love They Are, and have Always Been. Love, self Love

# A little footnote

I do believe and Feel deep in my Heart and Soul that no matter what I really love (and Love) to come and explore this amazing Universe we inhabit, this amazing Earth, our mother in this realm of the coming together of the physical, the emotional, the mental, the Spiritual, all at once! Michael once said that in all the Universes, Earth is the most "advanced" system. I remember when I first heard this I said, "No way!"... but it was explained that in most systems throughout our Universe and beyond, the lifeforms are "working on" one, or maybe two, dimensions, or developmental and evolutionary concerns; while here on Earth we have been working on all of them all at once for millennia; i.e., physical, emotional, mental, and Spiritual. It is the "fastest" evolution according to Michael, and requires that the Souls undertaking this be extremely "advanced." And he also said (and Please FEEL this, in your Heart and Body deeply...) He said, "Every being on this Planet is the most Advanced of Souls; otherwise you would not be here." With all that is going on right now, the trauma, drama, wars, famine, murders, hatreds, ..and yes, the tremendous technical advances, the metaphysical and psychic abilities that are becoming so obvious, the Earth Changes, the Love that is Pouring In from all over our Universe, from many Beings, and the Suns! ... on and on and on!... So, it has taken us many many lifetimes and many many Lessons, and many many Free Will choices... and here we Are! The animals who share this Divine Planet with us are profoundly evolved Souls, they are here with us in this profound realm of exploration. God Bless Them God Bless Us All There IS Only Love

# Bibliography

Alcock, John <u>Animal Behavior: An Evolutionary Approach</u>, Sinauer Associates, 7<sup>th</sup> ed., 2001

Bergler, Edmund <u>Curable and Incurable Neurotics</u>, Liveright, 1961 and 1992

Bergler, Edmund <u>Principles of Self Damage</u>, especially Introduction for those new to Bergler's works, Edmund and Marianne Bergler Psychiatric Foundation, 1992

Bishop, Karen <u>Heart In The Night: from Death to Rebirth</u> – experiencing great loss during the end times, <u>www.gamabooks.com</u>, 2011 (online orders only)

Brune, Martin <u>Textbook of Evolutionary Psychology: The Origins of Psychopathology</u>, Oxford U. Press, 2008 (in this work the author explores the evolution of psychopathology as actually once adaptive behaviors, which develop into non-adaptive extreme behaviors as the human race evolves)

Goldstein, Martin <u>The Nature of Animal Healing</u>, Ballantine Books, 2000

Himmelman, John <u>Tudley Didn't Know</u>, Sylvan Dell Publishing, 2007 (a wonderful story in which Tudley Turtle does not "know" that he cannot fly, that he cannot... but does it anyway! a very Feeling work)

Jung, Carl Gustav <u>Psychology of the Unconscious: A Study of the Transformations and Symbolisms of the Libido</u>, Dodd, Mead & Company, 1949

King, Soluntra <u>The Diamond Light Body Activation, DNA Integration and RNA</u>, online orders only at www.evenstarcreations.com. Also many resources on Earth Changes, Ascension, Sacred Earth locations, Star Portals, Essences, and a wonderful news letter

Losey, Meg Blackburn <u>Children of NOW</u>, Career Press, 2007

McCutcheon, Paul and Weinstein, Susan <u>The Stress-Health Connection: The New Holistic Way for Dogs and Cats</u>, Celestial Arts, 1st ed., 2009

Pitcairn, Richard and Hubble-Pitcairn, Susan <u>New Complete Guide to Natural Health for Dogs and Cats</u>, Rodale Books, 3rd ed., 2005

Roads, Michael <u>Into A Timeless Realm</u>, H.J. Kramer, 1996

Roads, Michael <u>Talking With Nature and Journey Into Nature</u>, H.J. Kramer/New World Library, 2003

Royal, Lyssa and Priest, Keith <u>Prism of Lyra: an Exploration of Human Galactic Heritage</u>, Royal Priest Research, 1989, and revised 1992

Sitchin, Zecharia <u>The Twelfth Planet, The Cosmic Code</u>, and many other resources (Dr. Sitchin, a Russian archeologist, has written numerous books on the origins of the human species as a genetic engineering experiment. These books are based on his translation of thousands of Sumerian Tablets and other ancient works. He died in August of 2011, and was only one of a very few people who could translate these works in his day. He covers in his works earth changes over the millennia as well as how he views our evolution as a species as being deeply co-evolving with other off planet systems. He has several editions of each work, so try to find the most recent)

Smith, W. Robertson <u>Lectures on the Religions of the Semites,</u> MacMillan, London, 3<sup>rd</sup> ed., 1927 (this monumental work studies the origins of religions as rooted in clan and bloodline, and covers totemaic relations between clans and animals, tribes and animals, as well as blood sacrifice of humans and animals and the evolution of this latter into ritual sacrifice. This work also covers the evolution of taboo – which means "sacred." And much more. Its profound effect on the developing psychoanalytic community of his day, especially as relates to the evolution of the unconscious content, is immeasurable. See also, below, the ongoing ritual of bull killing by hands of the clan/tribe rooted in deep archaic and archetypal past but still practiced today on Earth.)

von Franz, Marie-Louise <u>Archetypal Dimensions of the Psyche</u>, Shambala Press, 1999 (see especially Jung's definition and aspects of the Self)

von Franz, Marie-Louise <u>Archetypal Patterns in Fairy Tales</u>, Inner City Books, Canada, 1997 (see especially "The Tale of Mrile" for insights into the psychology of the magical divine double - children and others with one foot in Eternity, and what happens to them when this magic double is unLovingly destroyed)

Waeber, Rolf <u>An Overview of Extraterrestrial Races: Who Is Who In the Greatest Game in History</u>, Trafford, 2006

Weininger, Otto <u>Being and Not Being: Clinical Applications of the Death Instinct</u>, International Universities Press, 1999

Wilcock, David <u>The Source Field Investigations: The Hidden Science and Lost Civilizations Behind the 2012 Prophesies</u>, Dutton, 2011

Wingmakers, James of the <u>especially Project Camelot Interview with James</u>, PDF download, 2008 (I ask people that when reading this work, which can be extremely intense and perhaps disturbing, that if they become angry or afratid to please set it aside until not so reactive egoically to what James is presenting. This work is one being's view of how the human race was "made" and again genetically engineered and beyond is involved.)

---

There are innumerable and wonderful Online Resources for the topics I have covered in my book, please have Fun! exploring these:

Topics include: Animal Communication and Spirituality, Earth Changes & 2012 Ascension

Nature (see some listed below...) Ethology (biology of animal behavior)

Universe Series on DVD and cable TV Nat Geo Wild series on DVD and cable TV

Documentary Channel, Planet Green Channel, Science Channel, anything on HUBBLE!

www.evenstarcreations.com, www.SpiritLibrary.com, www.Lightworker.com

www.Wingmakers.com, www.DisneyNature.com (especially Oceans, for Feeling)

www.SongMagicNews.com, www.KaTaSee.com ("when we heal we heal all else")

www.NormaGentile.com (Sacred Chanting) www.SpiritualEvolutionoftheAnimalKingdom.com (present author's webpage)

Genesis, a DVD on the Evolution of our Universe and our Planet and its Lifeforms, Fox Home Entertainment, 2008 (this DVD is for me the most Feelingly presented on Evolution, while also holding as true as possible to Darwin's offerings)

Tippi the wild girl, Please see Tippi's Official Site www.tippi.org/accueil-uk.shtml

Eat the Sun, DVD, released 2011, a documentary of humans who are living here, incarnated, with the Sun's energies as sole nutrient

Eye of the Leopard, National Geographic, 2011 (this work of deep Feeling and Acceptance of Nature is the story of a young female leopard and her life... the combination of feeling and Feeling is profound and deeply moving on every level)

The Story of the Weeping Camel, Top Documentary Films, 2011 (Song as the Opening of the Heart to Receiving... a mother camel will not accept her colt, and with the help of Song sung from the Heart by the Shaman, the mother receives/Receives her colt. This modern day Mongolian Tribe activity of Feeling is deeply moving and is mirrored in the work by Michael Roads "Into A Timeless Realm" in which he describes the interaction in times long long ago on Earth of the Laplanders in the Singing of Heart Song to the Reindeer who will provide sustenance to the tribe. Also, of importance here, is to mention the still practiced tearing apart of the live animal by clans/tribes in ritual sacrifice... Roberton Smith in his work describes the prehistoric practice with nomads and their Sacred Taboo Totemaic Animal, the Camel. Please see www.Care2.com online for this and for the ongoing harvesting of Sacred organs and body parts by tribes/clans all over the world even today. These practices reside in the deep collective unconsciousness, and even conscious, Sacred relationship of the clan/tribe to the animal that is the clan and the tribe Guide. The blood and body consumption of these Sacred animals are the clan and tribe's source of Spiritual Nourishment and connection with Nature, Spiritually and at all levels of existences here. (Please see Jung, von Franz, Brune, Robertson-Smith books above)